Reconstructing Relationship
Higher Education
Challenging Agendas

Drawing on two international research projects, *Reconstructing Relationships in Higher Education: Challenging Agendas* looks behind formal organisational structures and workforce patterns to consider the significance of relationships, particularly at local and informal levels, for the aspirations and motivations of academic faculty. In practice, and day-to-day, such relationships can overlay formal reporting lines and therefore inform, to a greater or lesser extent, the overall relationship between individuals and institutions.

As a result, from an institutional point of view, relationships may be a critical factor in the realisation of strategy, and can in practice have a disproportionate effect, both positively and negatively. However, little attention has been paid to the role that they play in understanding the interface between individuals and institutions at a time of ongoing diversification of the workforce. For instance, they may provide space, which in turn may be implicit and discretionary, in which negotiation and influence can occur. In this context, *Reconstructing Relationships in Higher Education* also reviews ways in which institutions are responding to more agentic approaches by academic faculty, particularly younger cohorts, and the significance of local managers, mentors and academic networks in supporting individuals and promoting career development.

The text, which examines the dynamics of working relationships at local and institutional level, will be of interest to senior management teams, practising managers at all levels, academic faculty, and researchers in the field of higher education.

Dr Celia Whitchurch is Senior Lecturer in Higher Education at University College London Institute of Education.

Professor George Gordon is Emeritus Professor at the University of Strathclyde.

The Society for Research into Higher Education (SRHE) is an independent and financially self-supporting international learned Society. It is concerned to advance understanding of higher education, especially through the insights, perspectives and knowledge offered by systematic research and scholarship.

The Society's primary role is to improve the quality of higher education through facilitating knowledge exchange, discourse and publication of research. SRHE members are worldwide and the Society is an NGO in operational relations with UNESCO.

The Society has a wide set of aims and objectives. Amongst its many activities the Society:

* is a specialist publisher of higher education research, journals and books, amongst them Studies in Higher Education, Higher Education Quarterly, Research into Higher Education Abstracts and a long running monograph book series.

The Society also publishes a number of in-house guides and produces a specialist series "Issues in Postgraduate Education".

* funds and supports a large number of special interest networks for researchers and practitioners working in higher education from every discipline. These networks are open to all and offer a range of topical seminars, workshops and other events throughout the year ensuring the Society is in touch with all current research knowledge.

* runs the largest annual UK-based higher education research conference and parallel conference for postgraduate and newer researchers. This is attended by researchers from over 35 countries and showcases current research across every aspect of higher education.

SRHE *Society for Research into Higher Education*
Advancing knowledge Informing policy Enhancing practice

73 Collier Street
London N1 9BE
United Kingdom

T   +44 (0)20 7427 2350
F   +44 (0)20 7278 1135
E   srheoffice@srhe.ac.uk

www.srhe.ac.uk

Director: Helen Perkins
Registered Charity No. 313850
Company No. 00868820
Limited by Guarantee
Registered office as above

Society for Research into Higher Education (SRHE) series
Series Editor: Jennifer M. Case, University of Cape Town
Jeroen Huisman, University of Ghent

Published titles:

Culture, Capitals and Graduate Futures
Ciaran Burke

Researching Higher Education: International Perspectives on Theory, Policy and Practice
Jennifer M. Case and Jeroen Huisman

Freedom to Learn: The Threat to Student Academic Freedom and Why It Needs to Be Reclaimed
Bruce Macfarlane

Student Politics and Protest: International Perspectives
Rachel Brooks

Theorising Learning to Teach in Higher Education
Brenda Leibowitz, Vivienne Bozalek and Peter Kahn

Access to Higher Education: Theoretical Perspectives and Contemporary Challenges
Anna Mountford-Zimdars and Neil Harrison

Changing Pedagogical Spaces in Higher Education: Diversity, Inequalities and Misrecognition
Penny Jane Burke, Gill Crozier and Lauren Ila Misiaszek

Religion and Higher Education in Europe and North America
Kristin Aune and Jacqueline Stevenson

Reconstructing Relationships in Higher Education

Challenging Agendas

Celia Whitchurch and
George Gordon

Routledge
Taylor & Francis Group
LONDON AND NEW YORK

First published 2017
by Routledge
2 Park Square, Milton Park, Abingdon, Oxon OX14 4RN

and by Routledge
711 Third Avenue, New York, NY 10017

Routledge is an imprint of the Taylor & Francis Group, an informa business

British Library Cataloguing in Publication Data
A catalogue record for this book is available from the British Library

Library of Congress Cataloging in Publication Data
A catalog record for this book has been requested

ISBN: 978-1-138-81081-5 (hbk)
ISBN: 978-1-138-81082-2 (pbk)
ISBN: 978-1-315-74935-8 (ebk)

Typeset in Galliard
by diacriTech, Chennai

MIX
Paper from
responsible sources
FSC
www.fsc.org   FSC® C013056

Printed and bound in Great Britain by
TJ International Ltd, Padstow, Cornwall

In loving memory of Jane Gordon

If you get the relationships right, everything else falls into place
(learning technologist).
　　　(Whitchurch 2013: 63)

Contents

Figures and tables

Figures

Tables

Preface

This monograph builds on and updates material in *Academic and Professional Staff in Higher Education: The Challenges of a Diversifying Workforce* (Gordon and Whitchurch 2010), to consider developments that have occurred since then, both in the UK and worldwide. It also draws on the empirical studies associated with a report for the UK Leadership Foundation for Higher Education (LFHE), *Staffing Models and Institutional Flexibility* (Whitchurch and Gordon 2013), and a report for the UK Higher Education Academy (HEA), *Shifting Landscapes: Meeting the Staff Development Needs of the Changing Academic Workforce* (Locke, Whitchurch, Smith and Mazenod 2016). Although both projects were primarily UK based, both sought the views of international expert witnesses and commentators. These accounts, together with a reading of the international literature, have allowed an overview to be taken which is likely to have resonance in other countries, in particular the US, Australasia and South Africa.

Both studies looked at organisational structures, models and strategies, but also included qualitative narratives that give an insight into the hidden worlds of an increasingly diversified workforce, including those working on short-term and part-time contracts, those formally or informally restricted to teaching and/ or research, and those undertaking roles with academic components but not necessarily having academic contracts. At the heart of this monograph are the dynamics of working relationships between senior management teams (or in US terms, senior administrators), local managers, rank-and-file faculty and their peer networks. Such relationships appear to be increasingly significant in ensuring that all these groups are committed to institutional missions at the same time as fulfilling their own personal and career aspirations.

It is intended that the text will be of interest to both academic researchers and practising managers interested in higher education roles and identities, careers and working patterns, as well as in institutional organisation and management. To address an international readership, the term 'academic faculty' has been used throughout to refer to what in the UK would be termed 'academic staff'. Where there is reference to 'managers', these may be senior academic managers (such as vice-chancellors and pro-vice-chancellors in UK or Australian terminology), presidents and vice-presidents (who would be termed 'administrators' in US terminology). 'Local' managers refers to those in line management positions, which can include academic faculty such as deans, heads of school or department. Within schools and departments it can also include those with, for instance, responsibilities for teaching and learning, educational technology and knowledge exchange. It has also been seen as important to include individuals working in so-called academic 'support' roles, in areas such as student welfare, widening participation, outreach and community partnership, employability, programme design and academic literacy. Although such individuals may or may not have academic contracts, their interface with those who do is increasingly critical for managing teaching and research. People not having academic contracts are sometimes referred to generically as 'professional' staff. However this is not intended to imply that academic faculty are not also professionals. On occasion the generic term 'staff' is also used to refer collectively to all these groupings. In the UK this does not have the restricted connotations that it has, for instance, in the United States, where it tends to imply individuals having neither academic nor professional contracts ie those in technical or clerical roles. Thus although this monograph is principally about academic faculty, there are occasions when reference will be made to the implications of institutional policy for relationships with professional and other staff. Similarly, the terms 'school' and 'department' are used to denote sub-units in the academic organisation of an institution. The term 'faculty', as used in the UK to mean a disciplinary grouping in the organisational sense has not been used, so as to avoid confusion with its use in relation to academic faculty.

Grateful acknowledgements are due to the Leadership Foundation for Higher Education (LFHE) and the Higher Education Academy (HEA) for funding the projects on which this monograph draws; to participants on the University College London Institute of Education MBA in Higher Education Management for stimulating discussions about the realities of day-to-day working relationships; and to the project team for the HEA project, William Locke, Dr Holly Smith and Dr Anna Mazenod. Finally, we gratefully acknowledge the assistance of Professors Rob Cuthbert, Jeroen Huisman and Jenni Case who kindly read and commented on an advanced draft of the text.

Part I

Structures

Chapter 1

Introduction

In contemporary global environments there is a sense in which the academic profession is increasingly embedded within layers of relationships, within and between institutions, and across continents. Traditionally these have centred around disciplinary networks, but increasingly they reflect other activities, such as knowledge exchange and professional practice. It has also long been recognised that extended academic networks are likely to transcend the relationship of faculty with individual institutions. At the same time, however, within increasingly complex institutional structures, the perceptions of individuals are likely to be shaped by a local network of relationships, which can overlay formal reporting lines. The significance of such overlapping networks of relationships may be heightened because there is no formal, superordinate professional body across disciplines, such as those associated with medical, legal and health professions, with which individuals identify closely.

These various relationships are evidenced in day-to-day conversations, interactions and communications, across academic and social workspaces, on and off campus, and via social media. They may be invisible except to local actors such as heads of school and department, programme leaders, research investigators, and the colleagues with whom they interact. They may be discretionary or even serendipitous, but nevertheless are a critical factor in the realisation of strategic intentions, with the potential for both positive and negative effects on the goals of an institution or section of an institution. This monograph aims to demonstrate that although facilitative relationships may be seen simply as a helpful addition, they are in practice more likely to be a pre-requisite, and indeed that a lack of such relationships can have a disproportionately negative effect. Furthermore, when relationships are not taken into account in the implementation of institutional policy, this can create what might be seen as a 'blind spot'. Relationships might therefore be described as the arteries of an institution, connecting all aspects of its activity.

Despite an extensive recent literature on higher education institutions as organisations and their relationships with states and governments (for instance Huisman 2009; Locke, Cummings and Fisher 2011; Pritchard and Karlsen 2013; Stensaker, Valimaa and Sarrico 2012; Stensaker 2015; Weerts, Freed and Morphew 2014), and also on issues around changing academic careers and identities (for instance

Fumasoli, Goastellec and Kehm 2015; Kehm and Teichler 2012; Locke, Cummings and Fisher 2011; Teichler and Hohle 2013), less attention has been paid to the different sets of relationships, formal and informal, that define an individual's positioning within their institutional community, and to the role that relationships (as opposed to organisational structures) might play in understanding the interface between individuals and institutions. Where relationships are referred to in the literature this tends to be in the collective sense, for instance between senior management teams and institutional sub-structures such as schools and departments. Moreover, accounts about the workings of higher education institutions tend to be viewed as cumulative, and to be judged in temporal terms, whereby change is seen as incremental or radical. Less attention has been paid to spatial relationships, including relationships between people, and the impact that these might have on institutional effectiveness, whereby '[s]ocial reality' is:

> made up of different and competing cognitive frameworks – discourses, normative and symbolic structures, frames and master frames, repertoires, modes of legitimation and cultural models – which create the social world in situations of contestation. (Delanty 2005: 145)

Although this approach has to some extent been explored in the way that individuals construct their identity by situating themselves in relation to others (Delanty 2008; Taylor 2008), it could be pushed further to reveal, for instance, interstitial and often implicit spaces in which negotiation and influence occur, underlying assumptions informing day-to-day interactions, and the collective impact of these on institutional life. Such an approach helps to bring into view the extent of individual agency in relationships and the social capital that may accrue from them, as well as the role of key actors such as, for instance, heads of school and department, in influencing local perceptions of policy and the way that it is experienced. Therefore an exploration of relationships may help to illuminate understandings about an increasingly diversified workforce, with links across disciplines and practitioner settings, internal and external partners and networks, and provide another dimension to cumulative and longitudinal accounts of identities, roles and careers.

The significance of relationships, which may not be articulated in organisation charts or job descriptions, can also be seen through the lens of social capital (Bourdieu 1988, 1993) and actor-network theory (Engeström 2005a and 2005b) to illustrate how practitioners interact, support and learn from each other. Social capital is created that would not exist if individuals operated independently, and has been described as:

> the sum of the resources, actual or virtual, that accrue to an individual or a group by virtue of possessing a durable network of more or less institutionalized relationships of mutual acquaintance and recognition. (Bourdieu and Wacquant 1992: 192)

This is particularly significant in complex institutions such as universities, where relationships develop across disciplinary and other domains of activity, internal and external. In turn, actor-network theory demonstrates how systems, be they mechanical or social, may appear on the surface to be working in an orderly manner while being subject to other dynamics arising from the connections between human beings and the artefacts with which they interact.

Although social capital has always been a significant element in the interactions within traditional communities of scholars, the narratives in the study suggest that it may be being constructed in different ways and for different purposes in an environment that is at the same time both more market-oriented and more regulated. There is a sense of making the invisible visible, the implicit explicit, and of unmasking day-to-day interactions within a collective that may not be as coherent as it appears. Thus institutional managers and faculty, individually and collectively, may have a range of perceptions that are influenced by local relationships. In turn, these relationships are dynamic and may shift along a spectrum that includes both co-operative and competitive activity, and are continuously remade. Such relationships may also influence how far the individual identifies with the collective and vice versa.

Individual faculty tend to be categorised formally, in national and institutional datasets, in relation to their discipline, career stage, teaching and/or research focus, and type of institution. At an institutional level, individual roles are framed by institutional structures, for instance formal terms and conditions, criteria for promotion, and workload models. This process is informed by day-to-day relationships, which may be hidden from official view, not fully or only partly articulated, and may be more fluid and open-ended than those described in job descriptions and organisation charts. The relationship between individuals and the institution is, therefore, to a greater or lesser extent, informed by relationships at a local level.

Moreover, as institutions become more complex and diffuse, and working life more dispersed, day-to-day relationships may assume greater significance for the individual in understanding what they perceive the institution to be 'about', and their own positioning within it. Thus notions of institutional mission are interpreted by the individual in relation to their own goals, expectations and aspirations, and may in turn be modified both at a local and corporate level to reflect the potentials and achievements of individuals. Low turnover in some institutions means that local relationships become even more significant. The interface between the individual and the institution, therefore, is a dynamic one, reflecting the ebb and flow of multiple relationships, with associated influences and counter-influences. These might be referred to as the cross-currents of academic life.

UK national and regional contexts

Since Gordon and Whitchurch (2010), the 2011 White Paper in the UK (Department for Business, Education and Skills 2011) placed increased emphasis on the idea of higher education as a market, with the Higher Education Funding Council for England (HEFCE) funding for teaching being replaced by student fees (except for high cost subjects, including science, technology, engineering and mathematics [STEM]) (Department for Business, Education and Skills 2011; Brown and Carasso 2013). In 2013 the cap on student numbers (ie student quotas for publicly funded institutions) was removed to encourage universities to compete for students (Crawford 2012; Callender and Scott 2013). Public funding for research has also become increasingly dependent on success in the Research Evaluation Framework (HEFCE 2014), and there has been a shift from higher education being seen as a public good to a service or product operating in a global market environment, with a consequent emphasis on the student experience and high performance in research. This also includes an underpinning of the curriculum by research that links into professional practice and employability agendas. At the same time, the proposed introduction of a Teaching Evaluation Framework (Department for Business, Innovation and Skills 2016), in parallel to the Research Evaluation Framework, will increase accountability requirements, and the 2011 White Paper also enabled a wider range of private providers to enter the system.

In the UK, institutions are also under pressure to respond to external drivers such as demand for a widening of participation in higher education, expectations of more flexible modes of delivery, the integration of employability skills into the curriculum, and participation in knowledge exchange and regional agendas. HEFCE (PA Consulting) outlined key challenges for institutions as being an increasing diversity of mission and strategy, with a move towards more collaborative models of teaching, research and service delivery; capability to deliver a range of activity; and a consequent diversity in future workforce requirements involving a need for agility and flexibility, seeing these as likely to challenge standard terms of employment (2010: 1–2). Universities may compete with each other for students and research and consultancy funding, but also collaborate via partnerships and consortia in relation to, for instance, library and IT provision, and the sharing of teaching. Overseas campuses add another dimension, involving local and/or 'flying' faculty from the home country. All these factors have had an impact on the role of academic faculty, with greater attention being given to the contribution that each individual makes to teaching, research and/or knowledge exchange, often calculated according to workload allocation formulae.

Internationally, governments continue to seek to widen participation in pursuit of socio-economic agendas as systems of mass higher education develop, leading to increased focus on the student experience. The Changing Academic Profession (CAP) study also lists internationalisation, a strengthening of management functions and increased value placed on the impact of research as key influences on academic roles (Teichler, Arimoto and Cummings 2013). Thus:

> The university as a collegial system is turning more and more into an organisation where different actors are involved … differentiated roles and positions

are created and new paths are experimented with to manage the variety of human resources. (Fumasoli, Goastellec and Kehm 2015: 204)

Commentators have also argued that the university of the future is likely to include the production of knowledge via both pure (Mode 1) and applied (Mode 2) research, involve external partners, and serve both business and community interests. It will therefore be increasingly global, with diversifying roles for academic faculty and students in online environments. It has also been suggested that second and third careers will become increasingly common, and that mass higher education will require a wider range of teachers for students who are less well qualified, and in order to address employability agendas (for instance Blass, Jasman and Shelley 2010). Such drivers represent a mix of both market and public service imperatives.

However, despite well-documented external pressures to become more adaptive, national agreements and codes of practice are not necessarily designed to address local considerations, and institutions have been left by and large to determine their own ways of doing things in ways that are appropriate for them. This monograph therefore focuses on institutional rather than national policy frameworks. It considers ways in which institutions are addressing challenges in what are often devolved organisational structures with distributed management responsibilities, what seems to work, and how rank-and-file academic faculty might buy into, but also influence, this.

Institutional contexts

It is a truism that higher education is a people-intensive business. In the UK, for instance, 54.9% of institutions' expenditure was on staff costs in 2014/15 (HESA 2016). Some institutions spend significantly more than this. Formal contractual arrangements for academic faculty are negotiated with the University and Colleges Employers Association within a National Framework Agreement which determines an agreed pay spine. In accordance with that Framework, individual institutions can make adjustments, for instance in relation to discretionary increments. In practice, and with no prescribed hours in their contracts, faculty have traditionally been flexible in the way that they approach their roles, often as a result of informal agreements with colleagues and line managers. Within their institution they may interact with committees and working groups, heads of schools and department, deans, directors of teaching and research, principal investigators, programme leaders, co-supervisors of students, line managers and mentors, as well as internal peer groups, teams and networks.

In England, the raising of tuition fees to up to £9000 per annum in 2012 has reinforced a market environment in which students have choice and expect a high quality experience, including teaching, academic and social facilities. Effectively this means that in the UK the funding streams for teaching and research have been separated, which may have reduced the possibility for cross-subsidy, either explicitly or implicitly. Another critical effect has been an increase in teaching-only appointments, for instance to cater for practitioner programmes that attract large numbers of students. Thus, on the one hand there is increased specificity, for instance in relation to criteria associated with teaching and research, and on the other hand a search for greater flexibility to meet changing needs and peaks and troughs in demand. At the same time individuals may seek to accommodate work–life balance, dual careers, caring responsibilities and other lifestyle requirements. Local managers are tasked with finding ways of accommodating these top down and bottom up drivers.

Triggers for a diversification of roles and relationships include the changing disciplinary base of many institutions so as to incorporate, for instance, health, social care, and practitioner subjects such as media and the creative arts. These may well be externally accredited, and involve collaboration with employers, partners and agencies, as well as teaching off-campus in practice settings. Such disciplines may have different concepts of what constitutes applied research from those in traditional, mainstream disciplines, and may expect different criteria for recruitment and progression. The tensions on institutions, and the faculty and professional staff within them, arising from, on the one hand, increased fluidity of roles and identities, and on the other hand from more regulated systems, are encapsulated as follows:

> Academics exist in a working environment in which boundaries have loosened or are perpetually shifting and there are different orders of space, macro and micro, which they have to hold in mind and which materially affect their practices ... Higher education institutions are more structured and more powerful and academic lives more regulated. Institutional futures are substantially shaped by economic and reputational competition, fed by national and international performance measurement and ranking. Labour markets are increasingly competitive and academic career trajectories are subject to more rigid temporal and performative frameworks.
> (Henkel 2012: 173)

The system, and individual institutions, are now so complex that 'one-size-fits-all' people policies are unlikely to meet the range of institutional agendas, particularly where student demand is uneven. Thus, in the UK, HEFCE has suggested that:

> The patterns and focus of future demand for different academic and professional skills will vary widely among institutions, and may be articulated in terms quite different from current roles and job descriptions ... institutional strategies and business models, and the workforce capabilities needed to sustain them, will be subject to continuous challenge and review, and must embody agility and flexibility to adapt to new conditions and demands.
> (HEFCE [PA Consulting] 2010: 2)

In developing innovative practices, institutions are taking account of a range of variables including balance of teaching, research and knowledge exchange; staff and student mix; size; locale and modes of study. Mechanisms such as annualised contracts whereby individuals' hours can be varied to meet peaks and troughs in demand; the use of hourly paid staff in relation to employability agendas and work-based learning; and departmental workload models are all used to adjust institutional provision according to ongoing circumstances.

Middlehurst summarises the range of possible responses by institutions to contextual factors as being tactical, adaptive and regenerative (Middlehurst 2010a: 78). While tactical approaches consist mainly of tighter budgetary controls, adaptive approaches include mechanisms such as redefining contracts and pension arrangements, organisational restructuring, and the outsourcing of some services to private providers. Regenerative approaches might include, for instance, a broadening of career progression routes, professional development, and working with partners on specific initiatives such as regional priorities. A key dimension of the latter approach might be seen as investing in human capital, and goes some way to acknowledging the importance of a focus on people as opposed to structures and processes. The chapters that follow take this a step further to consider the influence of relationships between people, and ways in which these might be seen as regenerative, for instance by being a catalyst in releasing individual potential.

Local managers such as heads of school or department are likely to have responsibility for managing the interface between institutional policy and the practical aspects of its implementation, including the potential for disconnect between the two. These two strands represent key components of the psychological contract whereby employers are expected, on the one hand, to provide a legal agreement representing an economic exchange in the labour market, and on the other to observe unwritten understandings about expectations and obligations on the part of both employer and employees. Formal obligations are likely to be articulated via job specifications, and informal understandings via the day-to-day relationship between line managers and staff. Local managers therefore have a critical role in promoting a positive psychological contract, which is likely to be based on a negotiated relationship involving 'social as well as economic exchange' (Cullinane and Dundon 2006: 114). This includes expectations on both sides that are not written into formal contracts.

The interpretation of institutional policies and structures is likely to be a major element in faculty engagement, including motivational factors and processes of staff review and progression, and there may be day-to-day tensions between institutional and individual ambitions. Although different traditions exist in different countries around employment relationships, whereby for instance faculty may be employed directly by government and have a status similar to civil servants, some of the general trends emerging from the studies would appear to be universal in that they are a result of a bottom up pressure from faculty themselves, for instance for more flexible life- and work-styles. There may however be a difference in the extent to which institutions have a degree of freedom to interpret such pressures and mediate these in their policies and procedures. Another question that arises is how equity for individuals may be preserved while playing to individual needs and strengths. This phenomenon is not unique to higher education and characterises working relationships in other sectors and across other countries. They can be seen in the context of a move to 'flexicurity' employment policies that 'seek to balance the economic need for flexibility with a range of baseline employment rights for non-standard workers' (Anderson 2007: 113). The European Union has adopted this idea to optimise the development of the skills base, including flexible and secure contractual arrangements for both employers and workers, and lifelong learning strategies to ensure adaptability and employability. (EU 2008: 3)

The UK workforce map

As has been noted in the Changing Academic Profession Survey (Brennan, Locke and Naidoo 2007), the higher education workforce is becoming increasingly differentiated, with distinctions between the interests of staff who, for instance:

- Work in different disciplines (pure, applied and professional) and types of institution (teaching- or research-oriented, or both).
- Have part-time, full-time, open-ended or finite contracts; or work on hourly rates.
- May or may not have management responsibilities.
- Undertake work with academic elements but do not necessarily have academic contracts.

In the UK, academic faculty and professional and technical staff are all growing in numbers as clerical and manual staff decrease because of increasing use of technology, re-gradings to technical terms and conditions, and/or outsourcing of services such as facilities and maintenance, as shown in Table 1.1.

Table 1.1 The UK higher education workforce (Higher Education Statistics Agency 2016)

	2014–2015	2006–2007
Academic faculty	49%	47%
Managers, professional and technical staff	24%	22%
Clerical staff	17%	19%
Manual staff	10%	12%
	100%	100%

As shown in Table 1.2, among academic faculty there has been an increase of those on teaching-only and research-only contracts, and a reduction of those on teaching and research contracts. Teaching-only roles may incorporate tasks such as learning support, the student experience, e-learning initiatives, and various forms of scholarship, blurring into pedagogic and disciplinary research, so that even these roles are not clear cut or clearly boundaried. Thus a broader range of types of contract has emerged, including learning support posts, the latter having a significant academic component but not necessarily an academic contract of employment. Increasingly, those in academic, research and professional roles may have terms of employment that are not uniform. It can therefore no longer be assumed that all academic faculty undertake a balance of teaching, research and knowledge exchange or service. In the UK, the Higher Education Statistics Agency data shows that academics having teaching and research contracts now represent a minority (48.7%) of the academic population (HESA 2016). This mirrors trends in the US and Australia. The introduction of a Teaching Excellence Framework in England will reinforce the policy focus on teaching, potentially rebalancing the incentives for institutions to pay as much attention to the quality of teaching as to research (Department for Business, Education and Skills 2016).

In the UK in 2014/15, 33% of academic faculty worked part-time and 35% were on fixed-term contracts. Of those faculty on full-time contracts, 26% were fixed term. Among part-time faculty, this proportion rose to nearly 54%. Between 2011 and 2012, the number of open ended/permanent part-time faculty fell by nearly 16%, and over the same period the number of fixed-term part-time faculty increased by nearly 19% (Locke 2014; Locke, Whitchurch et al. 2016). This follows trends in the United States where the majority of academic faculty now have non-tenured posts. Fractional contracts are also increasingly common, whereby people may work on different programmes or projects for which they are paid from different income streams. Continuation of their contract is therefore dependent on the continued financial viability of the programme. Thus uncertain contexts with short time horizons are making it more difficult

Table 1.2 The UK academic workforce (Higher Education Statistics Agency 2016)

	2014–15	*2006–2007*
Teaching and research contracts	49%	52%
Teaching-only contracts	26%	25%
Research-only contracts	24%	22%
Neither teaching nor research	1%	1%
	100%	100%

for early career faculty to plan their careers once they have entered higher education, and fluidity of career expectations was a key theme emerging from both the LFHE and HEA projects. There is also evidence of crossover and convergence of academic, professional and managerial roles, with a blurring of boundaries occurring between these in day-to-day practice (Whitchurch 2013). At the same time, there is a trend towards greater contractual separation of individuals providing what might be seen as 'support' roles, from facilities management to language and study skills, some of which have been subject to outsourcing or partnership arrangements.

The composition of the workforce is also changing to include a broader range of faculty, who may move in and out of higher education from other professional and allied fields such as non-governmental organisations. These changes are likely to be ongoing as the natural cycle of replenishment takes place and as older cohorts of staff are replaced by younger cohorts, who may have different lifestyles and expectations. Thus:

> the speed with which these major changes are taking place also suggests that there may be generational differences; that assumptions about research productivity, teaching loads, remuneration and benefit arrangements, opportunities for permanent employment, and other key workload elements may be different for junior faculty than their more senior peers, and that there may be related differences in perceptions of academic work and job satisfaction. (Jones, Weinrib et al 2012: 193)

As a consequence, it has been suggested that this turnover is likely to provide the opportunity for new forms of contract, for instance:

> the retrenchment of permanent positions in favour of a temporary and 'more flexible' workforce. (Jones, Weinrib et al 2012: 193)

Challenging agendas

The literature reflects challenges to a number of agendas, arising from, for instance, tensions between a model of higher education as a public service paid for by taxpayers, serving national and regional needs, and one that is market driven and confers private benefits on, and is at least partially funded by, students themselves. This has translated into an increased emphasis on business and industry links, knowledge exchange and employability, and rising expectations of students in relation to the student experience. An increasingly mixed economy has resulted, reflected in a challenging of agendas within institutions around, for instance:

- The involvement of all faculty in teaching and research.
- Expectations that all institutions will offer similar terms and conditions.

- Linear academic careers with open-ended contracts (equivalent to the tenure system in the US) for all academic faculty.
- Understandings that academic faculty alone are qualified to carry out functions such as the teaching of study skills, online learning, and the writing of research grant applications, as opposed to academically qualified individuals who may not have academic contracts.
- Expectations that institutions will deliver every activity in which they are involved via directly employed academic faculty and/or professional staff, as opposed to a sharing of service delivery, for instance via employee partnerships, consortia or outsourcing.

Institutions are therefore challenged by changes in global environments and also by government policies, in that they are increasingly expected to be part of a 'national economic ecosystem' (UniversitiesUK 2015). However, they have themselves, in response to external pressures, actively challenged assumptions, expectations, and ways of doing things in adapting to more market-oriented approaches whilst maintaining core values. Thus, at the macro level:

> policy needs to develop a normative model more nuanced and more sector specific than is the NLMM [neo-liberal market model], attuned to the character of higher education and knowledge that would establish a dynamic of reflexive continuous improvement across the full range of activity in the sector. (Marginson 2013)

In the meantime, institutional responses in many cases represent work-in-progress and a means of testing out new ways of working. The studies described in this volume suggest that there are likely to be local and practical reasons for the success or failure of such initiatives, often based around workplace relationships.

Challenges have also arisen at the interface between the individual and the institution. These include the incorporation of faculty with different histories and career trajectories, for instance those with a focus on professional practice; demands for more flexible career structures to accommodate, for instance, uneven demand for institutional programmes but also the lifestyle needs of individuals; and pressures to achieve creative, yet equitable, approaches to an increasing range of employment packages (Gordon and Whitchurch 2010). Early career faculty in particular do not necessarily expect a full-time linear career in a single institution. Significant number of faculty enter higher education from a professional career such as the health professions or the law, others come in from business and industry and others deliberately seek portfolio careers, working for different institutions or organisations at the same time. As a result a broader set of relationships has arisen, associated with more complex agendas. Institutional and faculty collaborations are likely to include peers, disciplinary communities, external partners, employers, senior management teams and local managers, as well as students. They may take place across research and teaching teams, with business and community partners, and with educational, health and social care providers. In today's world some of these relationships and collaborations may be more virtual than face-to-face, across national and global networks of disciplinary and professional colleagues who may never meet in person.

Thus emerging patterns of institutional activity and academic profiles are challenging relationships between institutions and academic faculty; between local managers and those for whom they are responsible; between faculty and professional colleagues; and between academic faculty themselves, for instance in teaching and research teams. Competitive tensions may arise, creating complex and sometimes political elements to these relationships. In practice, there may also be tensions within staffing models that are permissive in relation to the contribution of individuals, allowing personal growth and career development, but also seek to optimise their contribution to the institution's overall mission. Individual institutions, therefore, are left with the challenge of how to achieve an appropriate relationship between a diversification of institutional activity and staff who may be supporting this in innovative ways.

The empirical studies

The erosion of assumptions about the range of activity undertaken by academic faculty in the context of government policy initiatives and international market environments prompted the UK Leadership Foundation for Higher Education and the Higher Education Academy to commission projects that explored, in the first case, changing models of employment in higher education, and in the second, the careers, motivations and development needs of a more diverse academic workforce. Both studies reviewed the impact of an increasing range of terms of employment, the emergence of roles focused on teaching or research, and a broadening scope of institutional activities, as well as ways in which institutions were responding, the impact on individuals, and the success or otherwise of initiatives taken by institutional managers and academic faculty themselves. Details of the studies are given in the Appendix.

The two studies complemented each other in that the Leadership Foundation for Higher Education study focused on organisational models of employment, including terms and conditions, career pathways, rewards and incentives, progression criteria, and ways in which local managers such as heads of department acted as mediators in interpreting them. In this sense it was primarily a 'top down' view, though with significant contributions from local managers such as heads of department, who were able to straddle the perceptions of both senior managers and rank-and-file faculty. The Higher Education Academy study explored ways in which institutions could support faculty undertaking a broader range of activity, collectively and individually, at different stages of their careers. It focused principally on the views of faculty up to senior lecturer level (in UK terms), that is in early to mid-career stages, therefore primarily taking a 'bottom up' view, although interviews were also conducted with members of senior management teams such as pro-vice-chancellors with a 'people' remit and/or directors of human resources. Again middle managers provided critical insights at the interface between senior management teams and faculty vis-a-vis the day-to-day realities of institutional policy, its implementation and impact.

Bringing the two studies together enabled consideration of:

1 The interaction between structures and relationships in contemporary institutions, for instance between contractual policies and models and day-to-day, local relationships between those with people responsibilities and those for whom they are responsible.
2 Gaps in understanding, even dissonance, that may arise between institutional policies and their interpretation in practice.
3 Relationships between rank-and-file faculty and local managers such as heads of department and programme leaders, and also with internal and external mentors and disciplinary or professional networks.
4 Ways in which local managers address the expectations and aspirations of individuals, working with and around formal structures and processes, at the same time as maintaining perceptions of fairness and equity and meeting institutional obligations.

Method

The profile of those interviewed across the two projects was as described in Table 1.3

Although both studies were UK-based, they both involved consultations with international commentators on higher education from Australia, Hong Kong, Ireland and the United States, and the findings are set in the context of an international literature. These consultations were either in person, by telephone or in two cases by email. Although some broad brush comparisons can be made between different types of institution, individual respondents have been identified solely by their career stage. This has been in order to ensure anonymity of both respondents and institutions.

The two projects used different institutional case studies, broadly categorised in Table 1.4.

A number of institutions had experienced some kind of merger, for instance between universities and colleges of education or art, or a transitional arrangement, for instance colleges that had become universities in 2004 and were in the process of acquiring degree awarding powers, as opposed to having their degrees validated by another, established provider.

For the purposes of comparison around the theme of working relationships, the qualitative data from both studies was re-analysed, so as to understand more specifically the extent of congruence between the beliefs and understandings of senior managers and those of academic faculty; the roles of middle managers as facilitators and interpreters of top down, bottom up dialogue between the two;

Table 1.3 Respondents in the two studies

	Senior managers (e.g. pro-vice-chancellors, directors of human resources)	Middle managers (e.g. heads of school and department)	Teaching and research faculty	Teaching-only faculty	Research-only faculty	Learning enhancement faculty and professionals	Expert witnesses and commentators	Totals
LFHE study	22	15	0	0	0	0	16	53
HEA study	14	7	9	19	6	7	4	66
Totals	36	22	9	19	6	7	20	119

Note: 'Senior managers' denotes those managers who were likely to be members of the senior management team. 'Middle managers' denotes those with local, line management responsibilities at school, department or programme level. Some of those in the 'teaching and research' category also had co-ordinating responsibilities at school or department level in relation to, for instance, academic programmes, admissions and quality assurance. Sometimes those who formally have a 'teaching and research' remit may focus on one or the other, and in these cases they are referred to as 'teaching focused' or 'research focused' faculty in the text.

Table 1.4 Institutional case studies

	Pre-1992 Russell Group (research intensive institutions)	Pre-1992 Non-Russell Group	Post-1992 (former polytechnics)	Post-2004 (former colleges of higher education)	Private	Total
LFHE study	2	1	0	3	1	7
HEA study	2	2	3	1	0	8
Totals	4	3	3	4	1	15

and the ways in which formal models of employment are translated into practice. It was therefore possible to 'drill down' into the quantitative data and documentary evidence to explore individual stories and shed light on gaps between perceptions and institutional policy and practice, on how individuals navigated the landscape in which they found themselves, and on what seemed to work for them.

Analysis of individual transcripts took place at three levels: the descriptive (for instance to identify different types of hierarchical and lateral relationship), the interpretive (for instance to understand the gap between formal statements about employment models and policies, and local understandings) and the conceptual (for instance to review ways in which individuals have become increasingly active agents, drawing on relationships with colleagues and networks). This process followed authors such as Creswell (1998) and Miles and Huberman (1994), enabling 'semantic' (explicit, overt) and 'latent' (underlying, implicit) themes to be identified (Braun and Clark 2013). This allowed key relationships, formal and informal, to be explored in relation to, for instance, discipline, links inside and outside higher education, and career aspirations.

Institutional policy intentions across the two projects were explored via documentation and interviews with senior managers and their management teams. Although neither project was focused on relationships as such, as the narratives were analysed it became clear that between the institution, its formal structures and the individual were a multiplicity of relationships that were often implicit and undocumented, but provided another dimension to thinking about the impact of models of employment and the development of individual careers. It was also clear that a perfect match between formal narratives, contained in, for instance, job descriptions, workload models and annual review documentation, and day-to-day activities, relationships and working patterns, could no longer be assumed. This enabled insights to be developed into what one respondent referred to as the 'lived reality' of working in higher education, and the fact that a range of perceptions create what one provice-chancellor referred to as 'multiple realities ... not just one reality ....'

Conclusion

Pressure for adaptive approaches to formal contracts of employment not only arises from increasing system differentiation within national boundaries and a concern by institutions to attract the best talent, but also from the expectations and aspirations of individuals in relation to, for instance, work–life balance, mobile working and dual or portfolio careers (Middlehurst 2010b; Cook and Daunton 2014). Institutions, therefore, are seeking ways of balancing external pressures which demand solutions within national collective agreements, where these exist, with local preferences. As they and their environments have become more complex, and their missions more ambitious, they have sought approaches that meet the needs of a more diverse set of clients, partners and communities that can be tailored to local circumstances, at the same time as maintaining working conditions and making best use of resources. In order to address such issues, the higher education sector has seen the emergence of more flexible staffing practices. Such practices include employment packages that incorporate qualitative benefits as well as financial rewards, and a broadening of criteria for promotion and progression.

In these contexts, institutions are seeking to establish processes that are perceived as fair and equitable, but also allow for variation according to local needs and circumstances. Staff are achieving responsibility for others at earlier stages of their careers and may have ideas about doing things differently, particularly where they have experience of other sectors. Thus, institutions are not simply operating in response mode, and some change may be generated from within, both by managers such as heads of department and those for whom they are responsible. The respondent narratives that follow therefore reflect not only the 'push' of external pressures on institutions, but also the 'pull' of changing expectations from a developing workforce. This is likely to represent a balancing act:

> HEIs have a duty of care to academic staff to support them in maintaining their professional development, by allowing some flexibility in work alloca- tion, while also setting clear indications of what the role expectations are within the organisation … including the maintenance of subject status, new types of students, research and 'engagement' partnerships. (Rothwell and Rothwell 2014: 136)

Getting the balance right at institutional and local levels is likely to require fine-grained judgments on an ongoing basis and in the light of changing sets of circumstances. Therefore, alongside well-documented accounts of a decline of collegiality in favour of more 'managerial' approaches, for instance, Deem, Hillyard and Reed (2007), the LFHE and HEA studies suggest that new, collaborative, spaces for negotiation are opening up, particularly at local level. The situation is therefore more nuanced and fine-grained than would be suggested by a clear division between perceptions of the senior management team and of rank-and-file academic faculty. Thus Stensaker (2015), in noting that the concept of organisational identity may help to understand what he terms the 'university dynamics' influencing policy continuity, adaptation and change, suggests that more studies are needed to explain the 'intangible aspects of higher education' (p. 103), and to connect 'the "how" and the "what" and the "why" ... [and] the specific mechanisms that are at play' (p. 111). This monograph aims to make some of these connections through a focus on relationships and the role of individuals working at the interstices of institutions as mediators, interpreters and catalysts. At times this may lead to a symbiotic interface with management teams at institutional and sub-institutional level; at others it may lead to discontinuity and even disruption. Nevertheless it is intended to open out and explore what happens in these spaces and interfaces. Such spaces may well arise from informal understandings, but they can also represent creative opportunities giving scope for innovation and development on the part of individuals, often at the margins of formal job specifications. The chapters that follow therefore seek to focus on how academic identities and positionings are defined and influenced by the relationships in which individuals find themselves, and/or in which they actively become involved, considering the challenges and opportunities arising, and ways in which they are being addressed.

Chapter 2

Organisational frameworks

Organisational frameworks include not only formal structures and processes, but also custom and practice that has developed over time. The latter may be local to academic schools and departments as well as institution-wide, and in turn create expectations from staff based on what has happened in the past, for instance in relation to promotions. Structures can therefore consist of what is written down, for instance in human resource policies and strategies, and also of what happens in practice but is not necessarily written down. Because systems may be slow to catch up with custom and practice, individual processes may be worked around. Such workarounds may become accepted for the time being, although there may be a time lag before policies are formally institutionalised. This is therefore likely to be an ongoing and iterative process, particularly where boundaries are being pushed and/or bespoke solutions sought.

Institutional structures

At the institutional level, structures are likely to be influenced by history, size and location, key events such as mergers, and factors such as institutional partnerships and regional roles. In the UK, post-1992 institutions inherited a directorate model from the former polytechnic sector in which the senior management team tended to adopt a top down approach. In the pre-1992 sector traditions of collegial governance have been overlaid by senior management teams, often with devolved responsibility to deans and heads of school and department. This may accommodate more of a top down, bottom up approach. In recent years these models have tended to converge in response to the circumstances of individual institutions, influenced by a crossing of sectors over a period of twenty years by both vice-chancellors and senior managers (Shattock 2014), although as shown by Locke and Bennion (2011), faculty perceptions of a top down approach continue to be stronger in the more teaching-oriented post-1992 sector. At the same time, as institutions have become larger and more complex, devolved management arrangements have become widespread, giving more responsibility to senior managers in schools, faculties and departments for both budgets and people. This is of particular significance for relationships forged at local level between middle managers and academic faculty, and also between peer groups and teams. Local managers have a pivotal role in implementing and monitoring institutional policy, not least to ensure that unintended consequences do not arise either for the institution or faculty. This may involve being both impartial and sympathetic at the same time.

On the one hand, some practices have become more regulated at the organisational level (see for instance Fumasoli 2015). This has led to well-documented tensions arising from what is seen as a more managed approach and greater instrumentality by institutions in relation to both teaching and research, including the use of workload models and targets for publication and grant income. This may be perceived as compartmentalising activity, reducing synergy between teaching and research and discouraging interdisciplinary working. On the other hand, some practices, often at a local level, have become more fluid and open to interpretation by middle managers, highlighting the iteration between 'individual, departmental and institutional practices and approaches to clearly defined policies and strategies' (Gordon 2003: 96). Facilitating the connection between institutional policy, including legal and regulatory requirements, and the interpretation of these in practice, in ways that are openly communicated and understood, is likely to be critical to creating a positive environment for academic work, and require ongoing attention via a process of 'legitimising, valuing and aligning ... multiple perspectives' (p. 101). At the level of the individual, therefore, academic faculty:

> encounter certain freedoms that may engender a sense of agency (e.g. relative flexibility in choosing and organizing work) as well as constraints which may reduce a sense of agency (e.g. demand to publish, insufficient time to meet all expectations in ways each might like) ... a reminder of the tension between the intrinsic drivers of an academic vocation ... and the extrinsic drivers in the complex conditions under which academics work ... (e.g. availability of positions and resources). (McAlpine, Amundsen and Jazvac-Martek 2010: 137–138)

The more immediate task of accommodating this tension between individual motivations and aspirations and structural requirements is likely to fall to middle managers, and be key to achieving outcomes for individuals, institutions and their component parts.

Another result of devolved organisational structures is that responsibility for people no longer resides solely with a small subset of individuals at the top of the institutional hierarchy, creating a less clear division between 'managers' and 'managed' (although these terms tend to be contested in a higher education context). Such responsibilities are likely to be distributed across a range of locales including schools, departments, and project and programme teams, and expertise may reside with early career staff who may act, for instance, as team leaders in the application of online learning. Individuals may also be responsible to different line managers for different activities across academic programmes, teaching and research activity. Managing peers can be a particular challenge for academic faculty who may be in the role for a limited period and are therefore responsible for people who were colleagues in the past and will be colleagues in the future. This in turn can cause strain on both sides.

Institutional success is therefore likely to involve a partnership between senior managers, middle managers and faculty in creating an environment in which individuals feel that they can realise their potential:

> Creating a positive working environment is key to the future success of higher education across Europe … Those who feel supported at work will enjoy their experience, like their jobs and have high levels of job satisfaction (Taylor 2008). The capacity to form supportive relationships at work is one of the main features of productive work environments. (Clarke 2015)

However, uncertain environments and consequent pressures on institutions have created challenges, including an increased 'decoupling between institutional affiliation and significant resources', so that:

> The university as a collegial system is turning more and more into an organisation where different actors are involved … in disciplines where we find generational change is already at play among senior professors, we find flatter relationships, new career structures, independence through international experience, competition for international funding…. (Fumasoli, Goastellec and Kehm 2015: 204–207)

It is in these contexts that new relationships are being formed, including those with 'third space professionals' (Whitchurch 2013), who work between academic and professional domains in areas such as learning enhancement, academic practice and research management, and tend to be project-oriented. Such relationships are of potential significance in informing and influencing perceptions and perspectives, particularly among younger generations. The development and use of social capital built in this way appears to be increasingly critical. Relationships may also span different work groups and teams, internal and external, creating networks that may be called upon for the exchange of information, advice and support when circumstances demand.

The studies enabled consideration of the implications in practice of a broader range of structural models, and the changing dynamics of increasingly loosely coupled institutions. They also demonstrated the inter-relationship between relationships and structures, and what is often seen in the literature as a struggle by faculty against imposed structures. Evidence from the studies suggests that although often seen in binary terms, relationships and structures need not necessarily be opposing forces, and that institutions and individuals find ways of accommodating and achieving synergy between the two. These observations support findings in the organisational literature that despite the requirement for ongoing investment in 'informational and relational work' (Feldman and Khademian 2007: 320), both institutions and stakeholders benefit from the active involvement of the latter in policymaking via community networks (Benington 2011; Ferlie, Musselin and Adresani 2008; Quick and Feldman 2011; Denis, Ferlie and van Gestel 2015). This includes, in the case of universities, academic faculty, professional staff, and local partners. Thus Smeenk, Teelken et al (2008), discussing the mediating effects of local practices on faculty in European higher education institutions, found that in countries characterised by 'high managerialism' (including the UK), there was a positive correlation with strong institutional contacts (relationships with colleagues), the autonomy to develop teaching and research programmes, participation in institutional decisions, and a strong 'affective' or personal commitment to the specific locale in which the individual is working and social relationships within it. Furthermore, they note that in distributed and centralised structures, different sets of factors are likely to affect organisational commitment.

Similarly, Hendriks and Sousa found that 'the social element is crucial for understanding how motivation comes about and how it may be frustrated', suggesting that a major positive factor is the support of senior colleagues (Hendriks and Sousa 2008: 371–2). This is corroborated by Smith and Boyd (2010: 3) who point to 'the social nature of workplace learning':

> Teaching team colleagues were most frequently mentioned as a key source of support, 54% of respondents placed them as highly significant ... particularly gaining support from those colleagues with whom they share office space, a corridor or a coffee room. A considerable number of new lecturers had sought out their own informal mentor. (Smith and Boyd 2010: 10)

Although institutions can endeavour to facilitate the social aspects of an individual's working life, therefore, this suggests that there is also likely to be an element of voluntarism in this process. However there has been less exploration in higher education of the symbiotic relationship between organisational structures and processes, the agency of individuals, and the sub-strata of relationships that are formed day-to-day, and of possible dissonance between formal structures, terms and conditions, and day-to-day relationships that define the 'psychological contract'.

Academic roles

On the one hand, some academic roles are becoming more permeable and complex, with new elements or bundles of activity being added to them (Fanghanel 2012; Whitchurch 2013). For instance there is evidence of an extension of such roles via the incorporation of practice subjects such as health and social care, and the inclusion of activity geared to, for instance, widening participation, employability, internationalisation and regional partnership. These are likely to require:

> different behaviours and skills, with much greater emphasis on cross-disciplinary collaborations and responsiveness to funders' demand for 'useful' applications and solutions ... [T]eaching for professional formation will demand people with first-hand experience of 'live' issues and practices as well as pedagogic skills.... (HEFCE [PA Consulting] 2010: 4)

This may create stress induced by trying to cover an extended range of activity (Kinman and Court 2010), although in practice an individual may also be obliged to reduce their contribution to a specific activity, whether or not this is reflected in their formal job description. Such extended roles are also likely to involve extra-curricular or extra-disciplinary relationships, so that, for instance, people in fields such as knowledge exchange need to have an understanding of and contacts in both academic and business worlds. One policy report suggests that there is now increased recognition that:

> the institution must cater for academics with differing objectives relating to research, teaching and knowledge exchange ... Many HEIs recognise that some academics should focus on research and/or teaching and have less engagement with external organisations, while others can, or should, focus more heavily on KE engagement and relatively less on research and teaching. (HEFCE [PACEC/CBR] 2009c: 103)

These trends are corroborated by Kehm and Teichler (2012), who suggest that academic staff are adapting to changing environments in accepting, for instance, the relevance of knowledge exchange and also taking management responsibility at all levels, including in research and teaching teams.

On the other hand, shifts in patterns of academic activity have also led to perceptions of an '[u]nbundling of labour' (Coaldrake 2000), and segmentation of roles (for instance Rhoades 2007; Stromquist et al 2007; Macfarlane 2010; Teichler, Arimoto and Cummings 2013; Locke 2014). Some roles have become focused on teaching, research or some other activity, with contracts reflecting this (Locke et al. 2016). Thus roles are at the same time becoming more differentiated and more specialised, with the emergence of teaching-only roles, whether these are formally designated or not. As a result of this, a key structural issue has emerged in the UK, US and Australia as to whether all academic staff might be expected to undertake a balanced portfolio of teaching, research and knowledge exchange activity, or whether individuals should be encouraged to focus on a specific area that plays to their strengths and, if the latter, how this might affect pay and reward structures. The longstanding tradition of a balanced portfolio, with synergy between the different elements, was articulated in the Carnegie

Foundation international study of the academic profession (Boyer, Altbach and Whitelaw 1994; Altbach 1996). The notion of the 'complete scholar' (O'Meara and Rice 2005), involving Boyer's four types of scholarship (discovery, transmission, integration and application [Boyer 1990]), with synergy between them, continues to represent an aspiration for many, especially at the start of their careers. However, achieving an appropriate balance is likely to include negotiation with line managers in individuals' academic departments, and the determination of individual portfolios, which may change over time.

It is therefore increasingly recognised that the academic profession is becoming less homogenous, and that it no longer involves a single 'taxonomy of roles':

> the notion of academics as a 'cohesive group' united by a common pre-service socialization experience will become increasingly limited in its application to a shrinking core. (Finkelstein 2010: 153)

However, at the same time, emergent roles and relationships have tended to be under-explored and documented, partly because they do not necessarily appear formally in job descriptions, terms and conditions or career pathways:

> The changes associated with movement from the 'traditional academy' with its stress on basic research and disciplinary teaching to the 'relevant academy' are largely uncharted and likely to have unanticipated consequences. (Brennan, Locke and Naidoo 2007: 170)

This increasing range of roles does not map easily onto organisational structures, and efforts to provide a clear map of the workforce in any institution at any one time are likely to place people in formal employment categories that do not fit precisely, with descriptors that are relatively generic. Therefore a more nuanced picture is likely to be required, which takes account of a blurring of boundaries and overlaps with activity that may be undertaken outwith formal job descriptions, such as extended scholarship, shading into 'research', by those in 'teaching only' roles.

Career trajectories

This expansion and diversification of roles and of the composition of the workforce is also reflected in career trajectories. Individuals may be faced with decisions about whether to pursue a teaching or research track, to try to maintain a balanced portfolio, or to support the development of the institutional profile in an area such as widening participation or internationalisation. Management has also become a career route in itself for academic managers who may initially serve for a limited term, but then choose not to go back into mainstream academia. In practice, career directions may arise from a combination of personal agency and opportunity, but can create dilemmas, particularly in the early stages of a career.

Roles are increasingly likely to include knowledge exchange and management responsibilities (Clarke, Hyde and Drennan 2013), and as a result some institutions are introducing more flexible pathways and career routes for staff in higher education that 'provide educationalists, entrepreneurs, and academic administrators with an opportunity to participate on more equal terms with those following more traditional or balanced academic careers' (Strike 2010: 77). Thus new career models have emerged. These include 'parallel ladders', which allow for different career paths including, for instance, roles such as director of research, education or knowledge exchange; the 'climbing frame', which re-integrates different pathways and roles such as consultancy or leadership, and also allows for crossover between them (Strike and Taylor 2009: 194); and 'snakes and ladders', which involves lateral moves between activities, for instance, shifts from 'researcher' to 'engaged academic' to 'classic academic leader' to 'research director' to 'broker', and from 'engaged educator' to 'classic academic' to 'educator' to 'administrator' to 'education leader' to 'research leader' (Coates and Goedegebuure 2010: 25).

This expansion of career structures gives a sense of the mutation of activity that is likely to occur throughout a career, recognising that individuals may wish to pursue different activities at different stages, and that they may work with different teams and in a variety of locales. This reflects aspects of contemporary academic life such as 'academic citizenship' (Macfarlane 2007a and 2007b) and 'public engagement' (Watermeyer 2015), as well as other activities such as international teaching, widening participation and employability initiatives. Thus, it could be concluded that:

> academia is evolving, in response to the strategic, competitive, or organizational needs of institutions, to a new, diversified form that is less exclusive and recognizes different contributions and career routes. (Strike 2010: 94)

Strike goes on to suggest that changes in career tracks are attractive to institutions because they can be seen as both 'institutionally strategic and academically benign' (Strike 2010: 94).

Arising out of the Changing Academic Profession study, Finkelstein (2007), Cummings and Finkelstein (2012), and Fumasoli, Goastellec and Kehm (2015) have outlined key changes to academic careers, signalling a shift away from the Humboldtian model linking research and teaching, exemplified by a linear career track starting with a doctorate, and moving straight into a junior lectureship. In the US this would involve a tenure track appointment, leading to confirmation, tenure review, and promotion to an associate or full professorship. However, as a result of an increase in non-tenure track, fixed-term and part-time positions, the majority of newly-appointed staff in the US are seen by some as part of a separate, parallel system. Thus:

> a new 'model' or prototype of the academic career has emerged – or more accurately, a multiplicity of such models has emerged. While the tenure-based prototype continues to exist ... there has emerged a *parallel* system

of full-time faculty, term appointments that have become the modal prototype among new hires for more than a decade and, if present trends continue, will become the prototype of full-time faculty work. (Finkelstein 2007: 154)

Thus, findings of the 2007–2008 Changing Academic Profession (CAP) survey include the fact that:

> the last two decades have seen the diversification of a relatively homogenous and well-organized profession into a highly differentiated workforce with diverse work patterns, career trajectories, and institutional lives .... (Cummings and Finkelstein 2012: 13)

with those in tenure track positions more than twice as likely as those on contracts to be involved in research and publication. Conversely, non-tenured staff are more likely to have teaching-only contracts. Academic careers have therefore become less coherent or predictable than hitherto (Meek, Goedegebuure et al 2010; Locke, Whitchurch et al 2016).

As a result of this splintering of the single career track, Finkelstein (2007) predicted a possible model whereby in twenty years time, only 30% of full-time faculty would be tenured, and only 15% of total faculty (whereby 50% are part-time) would hold tenured or tenure-track appointments. However, the development of parallel tracks is not solely the result of changing institutional strategy. Lifestyle considerations, such as the fact that more women have entered academia, dual career couples who share child or elder care responsibilities, and pressure for spouse employment, have also had an influence (Austin 2010). In the US, the concept of 'professional school' faculty has developed alongside that of the 'arts and science' professor:

> Professional schools have always departed from the norms of the traditional liberal arts in terms of the faculty role and rewards; and only reinforces current movements towards greater specialization in the academic role. (Finkelstein 2007: 155)

Thus, a number of emergent career tracks have been noted, largely differentiated via teaching, research or knowledge exchange and/or community service. Linear progression over time in a pre-ordained career path can no longer be assumed. As Bexley, James and Arkoudis (2011), in an Australian context, suggest:

> A more sophisticated distribution of academic work roles than the conventional classification of teaching-only, teaching-and-research and research-only positions is needed ... the way academic work is currently valued is based on outmoded notions ... [new modes] are unlikely to follow clear career pathways, and may be comprised of punctuated periods in different work roles and even different institutions ... This process will not be

successful if a diverse range of contributions are not placed on equal footings within the policies and cultures of universities. (Bexley, James and Arkoudis 2011: 52–54)

Others have considered the impact of greater mobility between higher education and other sectors, and the forging of relationships outwith the institution. For instance Duberley, Cohen and Leeson (2007) identified two groups of mainstream scientists, one of whom moved in the direction of entrepreneurship and spin out (usually with significant 'career capital'), and a group of more junior staff who sought to capitalise on their scientific background by becoming technology transfer professionals. They conclude that:

It appears that an uneasy synthesis is occurring between a traditional, liberal model that expects academics to take on teaching, administrative and research responsibilities, a more reflexive model in which academics are charged with developing different sorts of relationships with the users of their products (be they pedagogic or scientific), and a more global, market-oriented model in which wealth creation through the commercialisation of science is seen as a priority. (Duberley, Cohen and Leeson 2007: 493)

Emergent models such as externally funded positions and cross or joint employment are explored by Brechelmacher et al (2015). In turn, and perhaps counter-intuitively in competitive and less stable academic environments, all stages of meeting the requirements for advancement on an academic career path are becoming more well-documented, therefore the academic career might be described as 'less stable but more predictable'. (Kwiek and Antonowicz 2015: 64)

A similar concern that has arisen, particularly for early career faculty and late entrants to the profession, is their transition into the range of tasks that faculty are likely to perform. For instance, Austin (2010: 30ff) identifies a lack of a systematic preparation for an academic career, workload and work–life balance, and opportunities for reflection and participation in the academic community as critical issues. Smith and Boyd (2010) and Gourlay and Sabri (2010) also identified a lack of clarity on the part of health professionals about their roles, and difficulties about the transition from a highly structured practice environment, which were not ameliorated by a 'superficial' induction process. There were specific identity conflicts for entrants who had transferred into higher education and also changed employer, as they encountered new sets of values and criteria:

The[se] lecturers seemed to be strongly motivated by nurturing students as new clinical practitioners rather than the possibility of making new contributions to knowledge within their professional field. They do not see strong links between teaching and research activity. (Smith and Boyd 2010: 9)

Socialisation into academia is seen by Archer (2008) as an extended process, with many pitfalls, particularly for those who do not feel that they fit established norms because of factors that can include race, gender, social class and age:

> questions of authenticity and legitimacy are central to the formation of social relations within the academy – with individuals and groups competing to ensure that their particular interests, characteristics and identities are accorded recognition and value … 'becoming' an academic is not smooth, straightforward, linear or automatic, but can also involve conflict and instances of inauthenticity, marginalisation and exclusion.… (Archer 2008: 386–387)

Gourlay and Sabri go on to suggest that facilitating transitions into the university involves:

> an expansion of repertoires … a notion which allows for a more inclusive and multiple understanding of these individuals' career trajectories … and the subordinate role of 'knowledge' in the wisdom of practice. (Gourlay and Sabri 2010: 2–3)

Cultural issues also tend to militate against women's employment opportunities and patterns (McAlpine and Akerlind 2010), summarised by Mills (2010) with reference to the fact that networking opportunities such as seminars often occur after hours:

> The seminar timetable and ritual are often sacrosanct, with intellectual debate continuing in a nearby hostelry. This nexus of alcohol and intellectual sociability may suit some, but not those with families to care for and other lives to lead. (Mills 2010: 90)

A recurrent theme is the priority accorded by respondents to having a balanced life, raising the question of how institutions can best 'respond to the challenge of helping those torn between the (over)powerful influence of a scholarly vocation and the reality of their working lives' (Mills 2010: 92). These trends and associated concerns point again to a need for support and guidance, as well as mentors, for those who, for whatever reason, find themselves in careers that are less structured and more portfolio-like than hitherto, with a lack of precedents or role models.

Furthermore, people having different career histories and trajectories are likely to have to collaborate in research, teaching and knowledge exchange teams, and to develop a *modus operandi* for the task in hand. This may require learning on the job and the development of a common language or discourse, if only for the time being. Successful working may therefore occur laterally and bottom up, and depend on local (and perhaps temporary) communities of practice (Wenger 1998), building on social capital. However the practical implications of these developments may not be fully recognised by institutions.

A 'core' and 'periphery' of academic faculty?

The introduction of more flexible staffing models has also been seen as reinforcing a trend towards the 'casualization' of staff as has happened in the UK, US and Australia, including short-term, annualised and teaching-only contracts, which are likely to have a higher turnover than permanent contracts (Universities and Colleges Employers Association 2013). At its most extreme this trend had led, in some countries, to the emergence of academics who resemble 'just-in-time knowledge workers' (Stromquist, Gil-Anton et al 2007: 128), for instance in Mexico, Brazil and Peru, who play little or no part in academic governance or decision-making. Assumptions about full-time, linear careers have therefore been challenged in the last decade, even in countries with well-established higher education systems such as the UK, the US and Australia, with more fluid patterns of employment being established (Locke, Whitchurch et al 2016). Part-time faculty include people having fractional contacts, which may be open-ended or fixed term, and also people having fixed term sessional or visiting lecturer contracts. Some may be paid according to work undertaken and have a series of fractional contracts with the same or different institutions that are related to specific programmes or projects (Bryson 2004; Bryson and Blackwell 2006). They are likely to include professionals in, for instance, the law, health, business or the creative arts and media who teach as part of an ongoing portfolio of work. Such part-time teachers have been seen as 'indispensable to running a complex educational and practice-relevant operation', and are likely to be involved in undergraduate and postgraduate teaching, supervising dissertations and doctorates, curriculum development and student support (Higher Education Academy [HEA] 2009: 2).

Faculty with practical knowledge in professional subjects bring expertise to the curriculum that might not otherwise be available, thereby enriching the student experience, and employability agendas have increased the imperative for this type of contribution. There is also some evidence that individuals seeking flexible lifestyles and careers, for instance with two partners working in different patterns at different periods of their lives, welcome a portfolio approach to work (Florida 2002; Meek, Goedegebuure et al 2010). Project-oriented types of roles, for instance managing a new employment initiative, possibly combined with work external to the university, may enable an individual to have the freedom, for instance, to run their own business (Martin 1999; Whitchurch 2013), pointing to the growing significance of social and professional capital developed outside the institution. There is also some evidence in the literature of a positive view of these types of roles by individuals seeking to develop their careers:

> Project work provided me with opportunities to engage with issues beyond my institution, to establish a profile and to research areas of educational practice ... Many people work on small, short-term projects ... These roles may be technical, academic, associated with support or professional qualifications ... This makes the networks beyond the institution immensely important as a source of knowledge, community and identity. (Pilkington 2010: 19–20)

Such individuals are challenging traditional career structures as well as expectations by institutions and individuals about what it means to be a member of academic faculty, and the nature of roles, careers and intrinsic motivations.

However concern has also been expressed that the use of part-time staff could have a negative effect on the quality of the student experience, for instance, the lack of a constant physical presence may mean that they appear to be less available to students, even though they may make satisfactory arrangements by appointment, via Skype or online (Rhoades 2007; Santiago and Carvalho 2008; Finkelstein 2009, 2010; Cavalli and Moscati 2010; Jones, Weinrib et al 2012; Cummings and Finkelstein 2012). In response to this concern, posts requiring some academic input such as tutoring and study skills, but not necessarily an academic contract, have been introduced to reinforce the student experience, particularly in areas such as widening participation and employability (Whitchurch 2013). This has again contributed to a diversification in the composition of the workforce, as such individuals may have backgrounds in, for instance, adult education, regional government, or other public sector bodies.

There are therefore significant challenges associated with increasing numbers of part-time faculty, both from an individual and institutional point of view, not least a lack of security for those having fixed-term contracts. Although such arrangements can provide greater flexibility, 'short-term posts are still seen as somewhat anomalous: a grey zone of semi-citizenship in the republic of letters, for whom permanent tenured staff feel limited degrees of solidarity' (Mills 2010: 88). Some may be paid on an hourly rate and be on an annualised contract, guaranteeing a number of hours per year but not precisely when these will be required. On the one hand, 'the opportunity to work part-time is clearly popular, but these areas of uncertainty may also create barriers to the extension of portfolio work ...' (Brown and Gold 2007: 458). On the other hand, these conditions can have a significant impact on an individual's ability to perform their role:

> being a part-time teacher can be an isolated and challenging experience ... 'part-timers' often have less presence in the university, have more restricted contacts with other university staff, less 'purchase' on systems for getting things done and less knowledge of the university's cultures. (Knight, Baume et al 2007: 428–429)

Furthermore, local managers are likely to have a significant role to play in accommodating those with part-time contracts. The same authors suggest that such transitions are best facilitated if the expertise of the member of staff is recognised and used ('Accommodation'), and explicit negotiation takes place in relation to their contribution, and the support that might be available for this ('Reciprocity'). Thus, an Australian Learning and Teaching Council (ALTC) report (2008) concluded that good practice was likely to include alignment and communication of policy across internal constituencies, with responsibilities for doing this on subject co-ordinators.

Workload models

The introduction of workload models is a good example of the inter-relationship between organisational frameworks and local relationships. Although one of their purposes is to ensure equity and transparency, this is not always perceived to be the case. Barrett and Barrett conclude from their multiple studies that for workload models to be successful, a holistic approach is required whereby workload allocation is connected:

> to a wider web of activities such as appraisal, activity costing and strategic planning ... there is still a need to particularise them to their contexts ... the head [of department] needs to retain a degree of discretion to make adjustments. (Barrett and Barrett 2007: 475)

Workload models are therefore 'part of a richer network of relationships ...' (Barrett and Barrett 2007: 475). They illustrate the delicate balance required between 'hard', technical mechanisms that demonstrate, and instil confidence about, parity of treatment, and 'softer' approaches that allow for individual circumstances and play to individual strengths. Their implementation is therefore likely to involve 'convergent/ technical' activity and 'divergent/social' activity, with a 'dynamic balance between policy and practice' (Barrett and Barrett 2010: 196-198). Decisions by local managers might include, for instance, whether to invest in the research potential of early career faculty or reinforce the track record of the more experienced. Thus:

> The allocation of time resources for research among individual staff members is to a large extent made up of compromises between different allocation principles, allocation criteria and allocation procedures, and can be understood only by reference to the historical and social context of each institution. (Kyvik 2009: 121)

If used in this way, it has been suggested that workload models enable universities to 'create strong socio-temporal contracts with their staff' (Barrett and Barrett 2006: 4), reflecting the broader claim that:

> managing change in complex organisations requires an understanding of the personal and structural relationships between the participants in order to establish and facilitate networks for open dialogue. (Paewai, Meyer and Houston 2007: 387)

However, the implications of workload models for institutional relationships have tended to be seen predominantly in terms of maintaining numerical parity between the contributions of individuals. In practice, the situation is likely to be more complex than this, so that within formal practices account needs to be taken of a multiplicity of local interactions and different types of contribution, which cannot necessarily be reduced to quantitative formulae or be directly compared at a single point in time. For instance, there may be reasons for a more longitudinal view to be taken, which emerge through ongoing discussion and recognition of the prospective development of an individual.

Reward mechanisms

In the UK there has been some recognition at national policy level of a need for incentive frameworks that will 'enhance innovation and creativity' (HEFCE [PA Consulting], 2010: 66), and reward contributions by those in more diverse roles (HEFCE [PA Consulting] 2010: 27–28). However, individual institutions have the freedom to devise reward mechanisms that are appropriate for their missions and that recognise staff who may be supporting a diversification of institutional activity. Thus, at the institutional level, Sharafizad, Paull and Omari (2011) found a range of flexible working arrangements including, for instance, long service and family leave, flexible hours, time off in lieu, working from home and job sharing. However, they also found that while there was evidence that such arrangements improved the attraction and retention of staff, take up of such options varied. In particular, although academic faculty were more likely to work from home and take paid study leave:

> their increasing workload has resulted in a situation where they can simply not afford to take up flexible work arrangements ... [thus] the attractiveness of flexible working arrangements is offset by the contested nature of the division between work and non-work time. (Sharafizad, Paull and Omari 2011: 46–47)

Therefore:

> the mere offering of flexible work arrangements will not ensure employee uptake ... A critical element will be to combat the increasingly debilitating workload and improve the availability and accessibility of flexible work arrangements to improve work–life balance. (Sharafizad, Paull and Omari 2011: 48)

Thus from a organisational point of view, the relationship between institutional strategy and appropriate rewards and incentives would not appear to be well developed, perhaps because of 'the complexities of operating a flexible reward strategy in a "traditional" culture' (James and Bare 2007: 12). There may also be a time lag in introducing appropriate mechanisms, for instance:

> While the individual academics involved in ... delivering offshore activity are enthusiastic about the learning that they have gained from their experiences, this is not shared institutionally, nor is it appreciated or valued within the institutional performance management frameworks. (Blass, Jasman and Shelley 2010: 7)

The Chartered Institute of Personnel and Development (CIPD) suggest that the 'total reward package' is likely to include opportunities for personal and career development, flexible working, being involved in decisions that affect how and when an individual undertakes their work, a pleasant working environment, well organised staff review processes, and recognition (CIPD 2011: 4). Similarly, in a higher education context, UniversitiesUK (UUK) suggest that:

> Pay is a significant consideration but other factors relating to working conditions, pension, administrative burdens and bureaucracy may become more important. (UUK 2007: 2)

Likewise the Universities and Colleges Employers Association (UCEA) states:

> Pay and benefits are an important part of the reward package for all employees, but research shows that individuals are also attracted, retained and engaged by a whole range of additional non-financial rewards from career development prospects and autonomous working to flexible working, work-life balance and recognition. (UCEA 2008: 5)

Strike and Taylor point to the fact that qualitative factors may be equally important to faculty as pay and conditions, and are more likely to be subject to adjustment locally:

> the policy agenda at national and institutional level, if it is to be grounded in the concerns of academic staff ... should be focussed less on pay bargaining structures or revisions to terms but on better recognition of disciplinary and institutional divergence; age, race and gender diversity; career planning and increasing workloads. (Strike and Taylor 2009: 194)

At the same time, from an institutional point of view, reward structures can also be a tool for rewarding those who help to fulfil strategic agendas:

> Academic communities on the whole favour the application of equity in reward structures, but in a period when competition between institutions has been increased and there is a greater reliance on market principles, a balance needs to be struck between collegially based reward structures and reward structures that recognize individual excellence.... (Shattock 2009: 73)

In practice, therefore, there is a balance to be achieved between rewarding individuals in ways that foster potential and career development, but also optimise their contribution to the institution or department. This is likely to require local managers to make fine judgements in relation to individuals, and flexible, light touch frameworks that facilitate sensitive and well-informed implementation.

'Human resources' as structure

The critical interface between regulatory obligations on institutions in relation to legal requirements and employment practice, and motivational issues associated with developing a positive psychological contract, has led to increased attention to human resources as a function. As with 'management', this is a term that has been contested in higher education, and is seen increasingly as something that is instrumental and performance-oriented, more geared towards structures and processes than towards relationships. Thus HEFCE (PA Consulting) point to a shift by human resources departments to a 'more strategic approach to business support', including leadership development, succession planning, specialist recruitment services and a range of remuneration models (HEFCE [PA Consulting] 2010: 25), although this may not in practice have had the desired outcomes. For instance, Guest and Clinton 'found no evidence of a link between more advanced HR practice and university performance', or at least not yet proven (Guest and Clinton 2007: 42).

At the same time, as institutions have become larger and more complex, with distributed organisational arrangements, there has been a heightened awareness among commentators of the role of local managers such as heads of department, who are likely to have devolved responsibilities for significant groups of people (for instance, Bolden, Petrov and Gosling 2008; Bolden et al 2015). In turn they are likely to be supported by human resource 'business' partners located in a school or departmental office rather than centrally. However understandings of this interface appear not to be well developed:

> Departments can be supported or thwarted by university human resources practice, although very little work has been done on the linkages between human resource and academic departments. (Knight, Baume et al 2007: 433)

Malcolm (2010) suggests that human resources practices themselves can be dysfunctional:

> consistent and auditable policies and practices ... dislocate[s] many university HRM initiatives from the everyday enactments of actual academic work.... (Malcolm 2010: 2)

In turn, local managers with devolved responsibility sometimes lack the skills, experience, and in some cases willingness, to address such tensions, for instance by investing in building constructive relationships.

However, the organisational literature suggests that although human resources is an essential structural function for legal and regulatory purposes, there are also ways in which it might be a catalyst in promoting positive relationships. For instance, Dowds (HEFCE 2009a) considered ways in which the human resource function could promote a qualitative and relational approach, drawing on international experience and practices in Australia, Canada, Germany, Hong Kong,

India, Ireland, Malaysia, New Zealand, South Africa and the US. These included the promotion of non-financial rewards and benefits, better provision of professional and career advice, and a greater alignment of individual and institutional development opportunities. However the focus of HEFCE policy reports has tended to be on leadership development and the improvement of institutional performance, although one report did highlight a key role for middle managers:

> Expectations of line managers to take responsibility for people management issues … are still perceived to be highly variable, even between schools, faculties and departments within the same institution. (HEFCE [Oakleigh Consulting] 2009b: 8)

This report also noted that partnership working could be more fully developed, and that the addition of professional staff with responsibility for equity and diversity and the development of academic faculty had been helpful. A further report for UniversitiesHR, the national association of directors of human resources in higher education in the UK, recognised the need for human resource departments 'to provide support, policies and advice to managers to help them improve all aspects of people management … [and] exercise a shaping role' (Holbeche 2012: 15).

The 'soft' aspects of human resources

When asked what the term 'human resource management' meant to them, MBA students on the University College London Institute of Education MBA in Higher Education Management in April 2015 listed a mix of what might be termed 'hard' and 'soft' management functions (Table 2.1).

The 'hard' aspects reflect those activities required to deliver formal legislative and policy requirements, and are likely to be managed at the institutional level by a director of human resources and/or academic manager with a 'people' remit. Academic faculty tend to associate these with bureaucracy and control, although those responsible for them would be more likely to see themselves as providing a service. At its least facilitative, this function was described by one director of human resources in the studies in the following terms:

> HR is seen as a referee and a policeman, as opposed to a change agent and a value-added supportive partner to the organisation.… (director of human resources)

Depending on the approach taken by the human resources directorate, and local cultures, the human resources function may be seen, therefore, either as providing a place of safety or as a place in which one is obliged to fight one's corner. Nevertheless there is also evidence that some human resources departments have endeavoured to bridge this gap by introducing roles that involve a more developmental approach, such as 'talent management'.

Table 2.1 'Hard' and 'soft' aspects of human resource management

Function	Hard	Soft
Recruitment and retention	*	*
Performance management	*	
Policy and compliance	*	
Pay and benefits	*	
Succession planning	*	
Equality and diversity	*	
Motivation		*
Well being		*
Staff development		*
Talent management		*
Organization development	*	*
Supporting staff		*
Employee engagement		*

The softer aspects of people management are likely to be the responsibility of local managers working within schools and departments who have discretion for implementation strategies and decisions within a given framework of policy and legislative requirements. They are likely to rely on interactions and relationships between colleagues that are more open and dynamic than those associated with 'hard' functions, though with the expectation of ensuring consistency of practice, equity and fair play. Achieving a balance between 'hard' structural factors and 'softer' qualitative factors in ways that are perceived as equitable is likely to be central to the work of all managers with responsibilities for people. Similarly, in reward systems, there is a distinction to be made between hard factors involving salary, bonuses and pension, and softer factors that may make a qualitative difference on a day-to-day basis, such as the quality of the working environment and development opportunities.

Between structures and relationships

Academic work is inherently messy and open ended rather than time-, space- or resource-bound, nor does it map easily onto organisational structures. Overarching policy directives, whether at national or institutional level, are unlikely to reflect this messiness. There is therefore likely to be an ongoing tension between institutions' roles as employers and as providers of space and facilities, and the desire of academic faculty to pursue their scholarly and disciplinary interests with relative autonomy:

> The in-principle freedom to research and teach as they choose means in effect that academic faculty have traditionally defined and owned their work ... To translate this ownership into everyday terms, when they are asked about their working week it is not unusual for them to respond that they have been very busy but have not had any time for their 'own work'. This is almost incomprehensible for those who define work as something that occurs in a time and place managed and supervised by an organization. (McInnis 2010: 153)

This illustrates the discretionary time and space that has traditionally been assumed by individual faculty. The studies suggest that this continues to be a prime motivator, even if it is regarded as something private and outside formal requirements. Finding this time and space could depend very much on serendipity, such as a chance meeting at a conference, or a special relationship, such as a sympathetic line manager or a contact made through an extended network. Institutional tolerance of this time and space, knowingly or unknowingly, was therefore critical to morale, and local managers were likely instrumental in facilitating permissive conditions, actively or passively, whatever staffing models were adopted.

The extent to which solutions are seen as imposed or initiated bottom up could also be critical. One reason for this may be that structural change alone may be perceived as breaching the psychological contract with individuals, which is likely to include local understandings:

> Whatever the legal contract says, you've got this psychological contract ... with the softer side of things, the spirit of the contract ... You cannot breach that in an organisation where you are relying on ... people to deliver [a] service. (chair of governing body)

This reflects research elsewhere that 'organisations ... need to accept the important role of "relational" contracts ... alongside traditional, legally enforceable contracts' (Sako and Tierney, 2007). Thus:

> it's not what's written down, it's the psychological contract that falls out of that and how that's interpreted that's the problematic bit ... When the contract starts to fall down ... you're starting to operate on goodwill. (head of school)

Nevertheless structural solutions are commonly offered as an approach to managing change, for instance by drawing together academic faculty and professionals in mixed teams to meet the needs of clients:

> Higher education can learn by integrating different staff groups in a single location (e.g. teaching academics, support staff, technicians) to serve their

student population more effectively. Examples might be locating business partners in an academic department, and common location of academic and support staff around areas of student interest. (HEFCE [PA Consulting] 2010: 77)

The success of structural solutions, however, is likely to depend on the perceptions and approaches of individuals and local managers involved in their operation. For instance, one aspect of the human resources function was its relationship with academic and professional development:

> I think at the moment, there's not really enough of a joined up focus with [human resources] and [professional development] working closely together ... There's a certain amount but it's very course driven at the moment and I would say probably not very well developed ... I think probably it's still seen as relatively transactional, not really adding much value (director of human resources).

Although in some cases the development function was located organisationally within human resources, purely structural solutions, without pre-investment in relationships, could give rise to a culture clash, and were unlikely on their own to ensure a co-ordinated approach (see for instance Gosling 2009; Moron-Garcia 2010). However location is probably less important than the interaction between individuals across the two functions. Often they come together in practice via line managers who are likely to be responsible for the annual review of faculty, and also for offering support and opportunities for development activity. A practical example of a mismatch between structures and relationships which was not uncommon was for an individual to feel that they did not have an appropriate line manager from the point of view of their academic interests. This was particularly the case if they were located in an interdisciplinary or practitioner-led field, or were involved in implementing innovative new agendas.

The challenges of aligning structures and relationships is illustrated by a sense that it may be seen as easier to restructure organisationally than to take a longer-term view about the overall employment proposition, including the way that people practices are interpreted across the institution. This is particularly the case if a new management team or vice-chancellor comes in with a brief to make changes, for instance by introducing a one-off restructuring programme. Moreover, whether this alters or maintains what one director of human resources referred to as the 'academic footprint' of an institution, this does not necessarily address issues such as fluctuating student numbers or a lack of critical mass for major research projects, which are likely to require individuals to be flexible about what they teach and/or work collaboratively in teams, or possibly in partnership with other institutions. Similarly, in an information services context, Law (2010) refers to the convergence that has taken place between library and information services to create client-oriented resource centres, and notes that restructuring alone is unlikely to deliver staff who are able to resolve user needs. Therefore a more realistic option has been to create 'small teams of experts each with their own set of skills, albeit still with some understanding of how to resolve issues in computing or web searching' (Law 2010: 191).

Whatever approaches are adopted, therefore, their success is likely to involve communicative relationships, constructed via an investment of time in face-to-face dialogue, reinforcing the view that relationships are likely to trump structures in motivating individuals:

> Leav[ing] time for personal conversations ... allowing time for what is really a personal process, rather than just an HR [human resources] process....
> (chair of governing body)

This reflects the comments of a director of human resources who spoke of operating with integrity and developing core values that involved treating staff with dignity so as to become an 'employer of choice'. Therefore the development of more flexible structures appears to be most successful where the institutional employment proposition is clearly understood, giving a sense of security and confidence to individuals, with good communication at local, as well as at institutional, level.

Conclusion

In an environment where contexts, as well as patterns of employment, are more fluid, making structures work is likely to require a broader understanding of institutions as communities, and relationships within them, including external relationships such as professional practice organisations and employers. This both extends and challenges traditions of academic collegiality and autonomy. As institutions and their environments have become more complex, and their missions more ambitious, techniques have been sought to address issues such as how to serve a more diverse set of clients, partners and communities. However, such techniques are only likely to work in practice if they are handled sensitively at local level, with appropriate adaptation to suit the needs of specific disciplines and cohorts of staff. Formal/explicit and informal/implicit accounts of the use of such techniques, therefore, may differ.

One key issue that arises in relation to structures is the establishment of mechanisms to ensure fairness and consistency, whilst maintaining a discretionary element in interpreting contracts so as to achieve individual solutions, where appropriate, to meet a specific need. Different models may be appropriate for different activities in the same institution. This reflects the findings of HEFCE (PA Consulting) (2010) of pressure on higher education institutions to enable more flexible working by combining different activities, working practices and ways of calculating hours; and to manage groups of staff on different terms and conditions, while continuing to maintain quality and standards. In practice, bespoke solutions tend to occur where circumstances make this possible, often at the margins, or as a result of triggers such as new ventures, partnerships or senior management teams. At the same time a cost–benefit analysis (not simply financial) is usually required at local level.

It is common practice for institutions and segments of institutions that wish to change direction to bring in a senior manager as a change agent who then proceeds to restructure the way that faculties and disciplines are organised. However, it may be more difficult to change cultures, which is likely to involve attention to the nature of relationships. Although structural mechanisms may enable institutions to make organisational and policy adjustments, relationships may be the catalyst for the internalisation of change, and may even modulate the structures. As one head of administration noted, although institutions may need to be more 'resilient and decisive', it is not 'just about decision-making', but 'the whole ethos of the place'. Whether culture is seen as an organisational factor that can be manipulated to achieve change, or as 'an integrated product of social interaction and organisational life' (Stensaker et al 2012), the agency of individuals is likely to be a key factor when it is viewed through the lens of a range of relationships at different levels across an institution. They might be described as the veins carrying the collective lifeblood, and when in a healthy state, stimulating development and promoting convergence of institutional and individual aspirations. Furthermore, a number of respondents said that the idea of the lone scholar had less currency than in the past, and that individuals were increasingly expected to have a profile in their disciplinary and institutional communities, at whatever level. Therefore the individual expects to be located within an organic as well as a structural system, in which they are an increasingly active agent.

The two studies illustrate potentials for the structural and relational aspects of the institution to come together in ways that play to the strengths of both institution and individual. They also demonstrate how maintaining an equilibrium between the two is likely to fall to local managers, who have a critical, and at times under-recognised and under-supported, role to play. These themes will be developed in the following chapters, focusing on the findings of the two studies in the contexts that have been outlined above.

Part II

Relationships

Chapter 3

Working relationships

Using the narratives from the studies, this chapter explores ways in which structures and processes, as described in the previous chapter, are informed and influenced by relationships in contemporary institutions, and vice versa. In each set of circumstances there is the potential for structures or relationships to either facilitate or override the other. Getting the balance right is a challenge for managers, particularly at middle levels of the institution. This might be said to be the junction at which top down, bottom up pressures can collide, and 'emotional', 'intellectual' and 'institutional' commitments (McAlpine, Amundsen and Jazvec-Martek 2010: 139) mingle. At the interface between structures and relationships is the psychological contract, in which local managers are likely to be instrumental.

In both studies, respondents pointed to the criticality of relationships between a wide range of staff and, increasingly, external agencies, as well as senior management teams, and the development of strategy in consultation with key individuals. A sense of partnership with local unions, or staff representatives in those institutions that were not unionised, also came through the narratives, particularly in relation to developing shared solutions. The psychological impact of change was not to be underestimated, and there was acknowledgement that people could quickly move from a sense of security to feeling vulnerable. Listening, empathetic skills and a willingness to spend time with individuals were seen as vital in introducing any change.

Devolved resource allocation and management within institutions has fostered flatter relationships in which heads of department and function have significant day-to-day responsibility for budgets and staff. In some cases, a deliberate attempt had been made to spread this responsibility, for instance, to programme leaders:

> [we're] putting the power into the course leaders to make the decisions about how they deliver ... what we are saying is that, there's your unit of resource, you've got to manage within that, and then they've got freedom with the course teams to make decisions ... we'll drive efficiency through that, not worrying about how many hours everybody's on. (dean of school)

This corroborates findings elsewhere that significant management responsibilities are increasingly spread across a range of faculty at earlier stages of their careers:

> The role of programme leader is not without its challenges as most have to deal with complex academic, pastoral, moral, administrative and pragmatic decisions on a daily basis. (Cahill et al 2015)

Thus, at a day-to-day level:

> I would always get my line managers with their team to determine what is the workload, including things like open days, interviews, everything that has to be done, and work with the team to look at how that is going to be managed on a reasonable basis. (dean of school)

It was also evident that those with devolved responsibilities for managing staff looked to the senior management team for support. Such support might involve, for instance, providing safe channels of communication and spaces in which discussion can take place. Several respondents referred to the difficulty of achieving congruence between institutional strategy and local implementation, and the need for iteration between the two, although there were examples of successful communication via, for instance, talks to staff, lunch meetings, surgeries, newsletters, blogs and online communication, as well as staff surveys to provide feedback.

The psychological contract in higher education

The UK Chartered Institute of Personnel and Development (CIPD) describe the psychological contract as being built on three pillars of fairness, trust and the delivery of the deal between organisations and employees (CIPD 2008). They also make a distinction between 'transactional' and 'relational' contracts. Transactional contracts are tightly defined and focus on tangible benefits such as pay and conditions, in ways that may form the basis of a legal agreement. They are more likely to represent a direct exchange relationship in which there is a *quid pro quo* between the individual and the collective entity of the institution. By contrast, relational contracts are more broad-ranging and diffuse, and stress the 'softer' aspects of the employment relationship, including opportunities for personal development, future employability, a sense of recognition, and work–life balance. They are more likely to depend on individual relationships and networks at a local and day-to-day level, in which social capital is built as an investment that might be drawn upon in the future. These may be exchange relationships, involving expectations of a *quid pro quo*, but can also comprise gift relationships in which assistance is given with no expectation of return, for instance advice, mentoring and peer support.

The relationship between transactional and relational contracts is reflected in Watson (2009), who argues that the culture of higher education comprises an amalgam of psychological contracts with different groups and stakeholders. The social aspects of the psychological contract have deep roots in higher education, and are central to expectations of academic autonomy and collegial decision-making. Thus it has been suggested that the concept of 'membership' is at the heart of the relationship between institutions and academic faculty (Watson 2009). De-motivators such as lack of autonomy, flexibility or feedback, or a declining institutional or departmental reputation, may be equally as significant as improved pay and conditions of service. Positive motivation may depend on whether benefits, including intrinsic motivators such as commitment to a project, are perceived to outweigh negative factors. Meyer and Evans also point to the difference between intrinsic and extrinsic motivation ie 'doing something for the love of the task *versus* doing something in order to earn some disconnected reward' (Meyer and Evans 2003: 154). They suggest that recognition by peers in the disciplinary and academic community is a greater intrinsic motivating factor than recognition within the university (although in practical terms the former is likely to feed into the latter, for instance via acquisition of research grants and publication of papers, and subsequent career progression). In contemporary terminology, therefore, the psychological contract includes ways in which institutions foster employee engagement, including motivational factors and the use of processes for staff review and progression. This relationship may be threatened when 'major change challenges attitudes, values or assumptions, and requires people to give up feelings of comfort, long-held values or beliefs and established routines' (Holbeche 2012: 14).

The push and pull of workplace relationships

Although the concept of academic autonomy remains at the core of faculty work, it is increasingly recognised that innovative and creative work is likely to take place at the interface of disciplines and between colleagues and partners internal and external to the university. Teams and networks, increasingly facilitated by the Internet, are key relationships for academic faculty, in which activity is managed largely by a process of two-way negotiation, whether or not there is a nominated leader or convenor. Within academic departments and schools, where institutional decisions and policies are implemented, local managers such as heads of department are expected to engage in dialogue with faculty, who have multiple and overlapping relationships, which in turn may overlap with social contacts. Their activities and relationships, professional and personal, are likely to flow inside and outside the institutional box, making the organisational interface a complex one.

Management or leadership of people in higher education is likely to involve implementing overarching policy or resource decisions that have been decided at government or institutional level, often with a tight deadline. These in turn are translated into action at the sub-institutional level. Negotiation and dialogue is therefore likely to be needed locally, particularly where non-pay conditions of employment are left flexible for determination by individual institutions. Even where trades unions are involved, informal meetings with senior managers enable consultation and dialogue, with ongoing negotiation and the development of mutually agreed custom and practice. Thus:

> One expression of this relationship [is] the common practice of presenting statements relating to HR issues as 'policies', or even Handbook 'contents' rather than formal agreements. (Stevenson and Mercer 2011: 12)

This has been termed a 'social partnership approach' (Stevenson and Mercer 2011: 15). Aiming for a stable relationship that is of mutual benefit, while allowing for pushback by either side, even disagreement and potential conflict, is a delicate balance, but represents a goal that is more likely to enable individual needs to be met.

Central to academic work (and other innovative roles in higher education) is the fact that thinking is essentially an individual process. This can lead to a 'splitting' vis-a-vis an individual's relationship with their work, between required elements that are likely to be specified in job descriptions and workload models, and more open-ended, creative aspects associated with generating ideas for new research or teaching programmes. They may feel more ownership of, and therefore a closer relationship with, the latter, and this may lead to a situation whereby they are:

> deal[ing] with two contradictory things at the same time without either transcending or repressing that contradiction .... (Bhabha quoted in Mitchell 1995: 5–6)

In turn, Meyer and Evans refer to Csikszentmihalyi's concept of 'flow' (1990):

> in which people become utterly absorbed in a task, giving undivided attention to what they are doing, losing track of time and space. People learn best and experience joy when they are in flow, and are unmotivated by threat of punishment. (Meyer and Evans 2003: 163)

This 'flow' may be stimulated by contact with colleagues and helps to explain why individuals may be unenthusiastic about the collective requirements of an institution, but more enthusiastic about their own project and local team. Managing this process requires an element of faith and trust on the part of institutions (and even of the individuals themselves), especially in the early stages of a career before reputations are built and public acknowledgement has occurred.

Measurement tools such as workload models, therefore, even if intended to ensure equity, comparability and transparency, may sit uneasily with the non-measurable aspects of academic work.

As noted in the previous chapter, the terms 'human resources' and 'management' are not concepts that resonate easily with academic faculty. This ambivalence, even antipathy, has been referred to as 'a highly resilient anti-management culture, even among managers' (Archer 2005). At the heart of this is the sense that high quality outcomes depend on individual faculty having autonomy and discretion over their work and factors that might affect it. People management therefore requires ongoing negotiation at all levels, often on a one-to-one basis. Moreover, senior academic managers with a people remit, such as pro-vice-chancellors and directors of human resources, are increasingly seen as having a more active engagement with strategy than hitherto. In the UK it is not uncommon for them to be represented on the senior management team, and to have professional 'business partners' who work in faculties, schools and departments and assist with local implementation of human resource policy. This not only raises the game for local line managers, but also raises issues about responsibilities and the division of labour on people-related matters.

Denis, Ferlie and van Gestel (2015) suggest that 'high end' autonomous professionals such as doctors are likely to adapt well to new practices and ways of working that are developmental and involve agency, initiative and exploration. This is also likely to be true of academic faculty. A focus on interactions and relationships, where multiple communication flows exist, would seem therefore to be critical in addressing issues arising from the diversification of the workforce. Although people management is often seen in terms of structures and processes such as recruitment, staff development and performance management, a broader conceptualisation would be to see it as a series of interactions and relationships as shown in Figure 3.1. On the horizontal axis are national and institutional policy frameworks, and on the vertical axis are the tiers of institutional management. Thus legal and regulatory frameworks and higher education policy flow top down from government and national agencies. Senior management teams interpret external requirements in creating institutional people strategies, at the same time as taking on board understandings of local practices and needs from human resource professionals and those working in schools and departments. The information flow is therefore top down, bottom up. In turn local managers both interpret and seek to influence institutional strategy for the benefit of their faculties, schools and departments, bottom up, top down. There is therefore a matrix of activities and relationships at strategic and operational levels. However, what has not been well understood is the way in which these local interactions and relationships interact with formal policy, and may be a variable in achieving new policy directions.

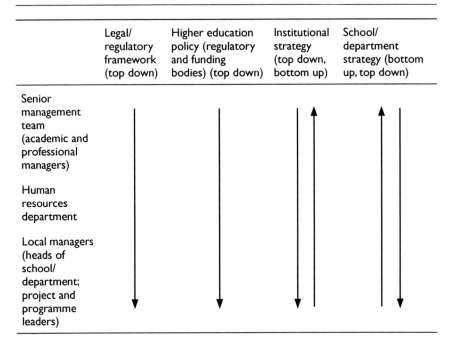

	Legal/ regulatory framework (top down)	Higher education policy (regulatory and funding bodies) (top down)	Institutional strategy (top down, bottom up)	School/ department strategy (bottom up, top down)
Senior management team (academic and professional managers)				
Human resources department				
Local managers (heads of school/ department; project and programme leaders)				

Figure 3.1 Formal organisational relationships in higher education institutions

However, institutional relationships are not only top down and bottom up. Those with responsibilities for people may have peer group links at local level, belong to wider networks, and communicate regularly, in person and via social networking, on a lateral basis. Project and programme teams may contain a mix of academic faculty and professional staff. Communication channels, therefore, may be vertical and horizontal, formal and informal, personal and virtual, with interactions between people at all levels, internal and externally. Thus managing people is not simply about interpreting policy documents, organisation charts and job descriptions in relation to those 'lower down' the organisational hierarchy, but is likely to involve a series of interactions that involve expectations, interpretations, and locally understood custom and practice.

There is therefore a sense in which working relationships have become less anchored in structures, particularly in a networked world in which they are no longer bound by time and place. Globalisation and the Internet have resulted in collaborations and conversations taking place across continents and between people who may never meet face to face, except via Skype, even if they work for the same institution, for instance on an offshore campus. There is a sense in which this has released them from organisational structures, and in particular hierarchical line management relationships. Individuals are able to accumulate and draw on social capital from other spheres, which may help them in a number of ways to build a profile, locally and globally, from improving teaching to winning research grants and authoring publications. They are therefore less dependent on the immediate physical presence of local colleagues, so that relationships have become more diffuse and characterised by 'weak ties' (Granovetter 1973), with a range of academic faculty, co-professionals and external partners. This extends the possibilities for 'just in time' contact, as and when the need arises, broadening the base for building social capital, as opposed to focusing on a smaller number of 'strong ties' at the institutional level, which may be less flexible and consume more time and resources. Individuals are therefore increasingly likely to maximise opportunities that arise through extensive networks, and to make their own futures in constructing a career.

Thus, alliances and influences may develop that are not necessarily articulated organisationally. People draw on different relationships for different purposes, for instance introducing themselves as chair of a disciplinary society, editor of a journal, or leader of a task force, ahead of their institutional or disciplinary affiliation and employment category. Relationships may be called upon for their significance to the job in hand, and although they may be captured formally in organisation charts, in practice they are fluid and shift over time and space, arising from and contributing to complex roles and identities. As institutions have become larger and more diffuse, local relationships, for instance with line managers, may acquire greater prominence and significance for individuals. In smaller, close knit institutions, or sections of institutions, it may easier for individuals to identify more directly with institutional policy because of shorter lines of communication.

The significance of relationships in establishing discourses that bring together strategy and practice was encapsulated by one middle manager:

> So there's that gap. It's not just the implementation gap ... It's almost a metaphysical gap between the language of strategy and the experience of teaching on the ground and in the classroom. It's notoriously difficult to bridge that, and I think one way of bridging that is to try and have people with lived experience in both of those worlds. (late career, teaching-only faculty)

At the same time a more agentic approach to structures was evident, with individuals negotiating the structural landscape in which they find themselves, with the help of line managers and mentors, in order to achieve an accommodation with the formal requirements of their role. This was nicely expressed by one early and one late career respondent:

> really it's all been quite clever circumnavigation to get to a point where I get to do the job that I want to do and do the job that the school finds most valuable. (early career faculty)

we have to create new opportunities, we cannot rely on tried and tested models .... (late career faculty)

Senior managers in turn are likely to be faced with reconciling 'top down' policy and market pressures with 'bottom up' considerations arising from a people-intensive operation:

the staffing is critical to [academic strategy] ... and probably ... more so than in many businesses in terms of relying on the initiative and the calibre of staff to deliver ... research activity, for that to actually feed into an independent curriculum and the external relationships the university has across a whole broad range of subject areas .... (pro-vice-chancellor, education)

This is exemplified by an ability to modulate requirements so that, for instance, appointments become a matching process, not overly constrained by a job description, that takes into account values and commitment:

around cultural alignment ... The right attitude towards academic engagement ... professional standards ... Someone who ... with the right support and challenge could progress .... (head of administration)

Although this example is related to the appointment of professional staff, it is equally applicable to the appointment of academic faculty, particularly if there is a desire to take a department in a new direction or to develop new agendas or partnerships. This also reflects Musselin's observation about the importance of 'criteria that are less "purely" academic', and 'social fit' (Musselin 2010: 136, 153), and acknowledges the interlocking nature of social as well as structural relationships. Nevertheless it is a:

constant balance between are these processes enabling you to find and appoint and recruit the right people ... are they enabling you to flex around the operational needs of the institution, or are they just creating a burdensome bureaucracy ...? (head of administration)

Moreover, recent scholarship (Crosby and Bryson 2010; Sun and Anderson 2012; Hogg, van Knippenberg and Rast 2012) suggests that generating a sense of collective identity is an effective way of pursuing agendas that serve multiple constituencies, as in partnership arrangements. Thus 'inter-group relational identity' can:

capture self-definition in terms of relationships with significant others ... and ... may revolve around significant asymmetries in the distinct roles and unique attributes that the parties bring to the relationship. (Hogg, van Knippenberg and Rast 2012: 238)

As these authors propose, this may represent 'an important step toward establishing shared superordinate identity – for instance, in the case of mergers ...' (p. 250). This could in turn help to establish synergy among a diverse workforce by:

> expand[ing] the users' behavioral repertoire through helping them choose actions that are based on more complete and locally accurate knowledge, while recognizing impacts on other individuals, groups, and organizations in the network. (Crosby and Bryson 2010: 228)

Although this may appear to be a somewhat idealistic scenario in what can be a messy institutional environment, the studies suggest that, as higher education institutions experiment with new approaches, a heightened awareness of relationships within and across institutional communities is likely to be a significant catalyst for success or otherwise, particularly in relation to development initiatives.

A changing interface between structures and relationships

The LFHE study explored ways in which institutions are adapting the formal structures that frame their contractual relationships with individuals. In order to achieve 'forms of governance and management that suit their particular mission and circumstances' (Locke and Bennion 2010: 37), institutions have responded to changing conditions by adopting a range of models. These often represent a balancing act in ensuring that institutional obligations are met, that they are appropriately supported, and that staff are motivated in achieving goals that contribute to institutional outcomes as well as enhancing their own career development. Thus:

> The employment contracts that have traditionally been in place in the higher education sector ... are inflexibilities to some extent. So from the point of view of the employer wanting to be flexible in offering a service, these are constraints. From the point of view of the employee, they are valuable certainties ... we have to look at things from two sides here. (chair of governors)

Consideration is therefore needed as to how to motivate individuals to be creative and innovative at the same time as calibrating risk, in the context of a range of institutional activity across, for instance, teaching and research domains, disciplinary and practice-based settings, and knowledge exchange.

The changing interface between institutional structures, and their collective relationship with academic faculty, is epitomised by three broad approaches to employment found in the LFHE study, categorised as *integrated, partnership* and *private sector* approaches (Whitchurch and Gordon 2013). While the *integrated* approach might be said to represent a traditional approach that may be found to a greater or lesser degree in a majority of institutions, the *partnership* and *private sector* approaches are emerging, at times experimentally, to different degrees across different institutions.

The integrated approach

The *integrated* approach represents ways in which institutions seek to align the contribution of individuals with institutional missions and values. The model is characterised by a holistic approach to role profiles, with recognition of different career pathways, although these would be expected to include either teaching and research or teaching and scholarship (including pedagogical research), the proportions relating to an individual's track record, aspirations and ability to win external grants, thereby playing to strength. The general expectation would be that teaching is scholarship- or research-informed, although individuals may have different proportions in their portfolios. Typically, an early career member of faculty, who might be appointed as a teaching fellow, would be required to undertake a period of probation, with remission of teaching in order to develop a research profile, before being offered a permanent post after three to five years, depending on their track record. This approach also included examples of chairs being awarded on the basis of teaching, although there was awareness that too many people with predominantly teaching portfolios could create pressure to either bring in more students or reduce staff numbers. As one respondent put it, 'we are research led and teaching excellent' (head of school). More than one person in this study took the view that there was no value in teaching being informed by poor quality research, or high quality researchers delivering poor teaching. In order to achieve a balance, individuals would be encouraged to raise their performance rather than to focus solely on teaching or research.

Under this approach, staff review, career frameworks, role profiles and pulse surveys were mechanisms typically used to encourage and assess convergence of individual and institutional agendas in developmental ways, with imaginative use of communication channels such as blogs and informal meetings. There was also likely to be a significant investment of time on face-to-face communication, by both line managers and representatives of the senior management team, in which attention was paid to promoting the institutional culture. Thus, '... significant work is done to help people understand their role and how they fit in' (director of human resources). To this end, and with the general expectation of a balanced portfolio, the focus was on playing to individuals' strengths in order to promote the student experience, research performance, and other key institutional activities, with strategy reinforced via transparency in the allocation of resources and scrutiny of vacant posts. In turn, the enhancement of institutional reputation was likely to foster the engagement of (particularly) academic faculty. Multi-skilling of teams was used to extend the range and quality of service, and a holistic approach to the employment proposition was likely to be supported by facilitative human resource practices:

> We need to be able to move [faculty] around based on need. We need to be able to shut down [functions or programmes] without necessarily making [faculty] redundant, because if we've got good [people] in a service that we no longer need, we don't want to risk losing the staff if we could put them in another place. So in reality what you want is a strategic HR function which designs flexible systems …. (head of administration)

The partnership approach

The LFHE study found that some institutions used partnership with other providers, including other higher education institutions, private companies and employee consortia, to extend their portfolios. Others had set up separate companies to deliver different types of programme such as foundation degrees, which allowed different contractual arrangements to be established with newly recruited academic faculty. Partnership arrangements with private providers included a range of activities such as language teaching, study skills, and provision of facilities and maintenance. While existing staff would be likely to transfer from the parent institution under the United Kingdom's implementation of the European Union Business Transfers Directive (The Transfer of Undertakings [Protection of Employment] Regulations), which maintained their contractual conditions of service, newly recruited staff would be likely to have different terms and conditions.

Some institutions had developed employee partnership models to foster regional agendas on employability and skills, which in turn benefitted the lives of employees, and also students via internships and business incubation. As one respondent put it, models that re-employed institutional employees tended to be 'for profit, but [not] for massive profit, they were just for making a living' (former vice-chancellor). The same respondent spoke of this model as a possible solution when, for instance, financial pressures required 'something half way between redundancy and the status quo'. Thus, an employee partnership model for the management of facilities and estates at one institution was wholly owned by the university. It was seen as being an accommodation between directly employing staff and outsourcing to a private company:

> There is a dividing line between getting something that is competitive … and the loyalty and the ability of the staff to … do anything that you care to ask them, whereas a contracted provider … would think twice as to whether or not they do anything but would think first, 'is this included in our base costs or something we would want to charge additional cost for?' So it's a different kind of model altogether. (estates and facilities manager)

This example of an employee partnership model for the management of facilities and estates was wholly owned 'as the trading arm of the university', with the aim of offering benefits from both public and private sectors:

> whilst value-for-money and cost efficiency [is] part of the mix, they're not the entire story. The other part of the mix is about delivering service levels and key performance indicators that are appropriate to the business. (estates and facilities manager)

The aim was to provide a higher quality student experience than in the past, and the institution would, at least in the initial stages, be the principal client, but it would be a more contractual relationship than had existed previously. Terms and conditions were likely to be varied for future employees so as to enable the partnership to compete for external contracts with providers whose overheads would be lower than those in a higher education institution. The company would also be expected to offer consultancy to other higher education institutions and to develop best practice. At the same time, if staff numbers needed to be increased at pressure points during the year, the possibility remained of bringing in externally contracted staff. The managing director was a voting member of the company board, a member of the senior management team, and a non-executive member of the partnership board, to ensure that the interests of both the partnership and the university were met.

Partnerships with private companies were mainly associated with freestanding functions rather than 'core' functions, such as student services, human resources and finance, generally seen as integral to an institution's mission. A consortium model included a variety of individual contracts but provided the basis for collaboration between institutions over teaching and research and the sharing of, for instance, library and information services and student management systems, as well as for services such as careers, human resources, and staff development. Such models could facilitate different employment propositions for different segments of an institution, according to local need and conditions. They also enabled the buying in of expertise in areas where the institution did not want to make a permanent investment for the time being. However conditions had to be right and unless collaboration was facilitated by similar profiles and business models, as well as co-location, additional overheads could militate against the value added. Above all, success often depended on local relationships. There was a sense that there was likely to be more loyalty and goodwill from staff who are employed by the institution, and this was often felt to outweigh possible additional costs:

> One of the things that comes with having your staff directly employed is the loyalty that that engenders. (estates and facilities manager)

Furthermore it has been suggested that the employee partnership model is more appropriate for relatively small-scale organisations that have well-established communication networks (Office for Public Management 2010a and b).

The private sector approach

The private sector model relies on staff appreciating the positioning of the institution, or segment thereof, as a market player, and being willing to contribute on the basis that institutional success is likely to lead to improved benefits for all. One private sector institution was included in the LFHE study. Other case institutions had established not-for-profit companies, owned or partly owned by the institution, to deliver self-funding, adjunct programmes including two-year/associate and foundation degrees, professional and continuing education, executive master's degrees, higher diplomas and short courses.

Common features include academic faculty employed on limited term contracts, who would be unlikely to undertake research, and on annualised hours contracts giving continuity of employment and pension rights. These options allow additional staff to be recruited if necessary on a fixed term basis to manage peaks and troughs in student demand. Some individuals prefer to have a portfolio of activity and effectively work as self-employed consultants, for instance in practitioner disciplines such as social work, media and the law. In addition, reward packages could be individualised if necessary, including market supplements, to attract appropriate and high quality recruits, and in some cases individuals might share directly in profits, for instance, from a high earning programme. Such enterprises could be located on a satellite campus, with library and IT facilities purchased from the owner university, and/or space rented on the main campus.

Under this model, staff review, motivation and reward mechanisms are likely to be aligned to institutional performance against competitors, with an emphasis on being able to respond rapidly to market changes. Thus job evaluation frameworks were likely to reflect the institution's mission, rather than for instance being based solely (in the UK) on the UK Universities and Colleges Employers Association (UCEA) framework. In the institutions in the LFHE study, there was some evidence of mechanisms more commonly used in the private sector being adopted. For instance, cost of living uplifts to salary would be included, but any increments were based on increased responsibility and/or performance rather than being awarded automatically year-on-year. Non-pensionable, one-off payments were also used to reward success at individual or team level.

The private sector approach seemed optimal when an institution or programme was perceived to be successful and staff felt that they had a stake in that success. Fees could then be charged at a level that the market could bear. A private institution that had been able to introduce incentive mechanisms based on institutional performance had benefited from the fact that staff had thereby received higher pay deals than would have been available via national negotiating arrangements. At the same time, care is needed so as not to have a situation in which bonuses for meeting specific targets lead to short-term approaches to strategy.

Table 3.1 Seven UK institutions in relation to the types of approach they adopted to employment practices

Institution	Pre-1992 1	Pre-1992 2	Pre-1992 3	Post-2004 1	Post-1992	Post-2004 2	Private
Integrated	*	*	*	*	*		*+
Partnership	*			*		*	
Private sector	*	*			*		*

Note: +The private institution displayed some elements of the *integrated* approach in seeking to align faculty to the institutional employment proposition, although research was not a substantive element of their career track.

Implications of the three approaches for relationships

The three approaches are not mutually exclusive and five of the seven institutions in the LFHE study demonstrated evidence of at least one of the three (Table 3.1). They therefore represented a range of possible permutations.

The *integrated* approach is characterised by an employment proposition closely related to institutional development. Dialogue with academic faculty ensures that they feel that they have a stake in, and can influence this. The *partnership* approach is, rather, based on ongoing negotiation between partners around the added value of collaboration over specific activities, whether these are employee, not-for-profit company, or consortium based. The *private sector* approach, in turn, represents more of a transactional relationship between the institution or segment thereof, academic faculty and other staff, based on a *quid pro quo* around competitive advantage, and a clear relationship between the employment proposition and reward structure.

The fact that the three approaches do not necessarily represent either/or options was articulated by one respondent:

> I think this binary split that has been created, which is big fat public sector with national pay bargaining and all that, versus slash and burn private sector that gets pay down to the lowest level ... doesn't have any relationship with the reality of the world. (head of administration)

Private sector mechanisms, particularly if deployed in companies fully or partially owned by an institution, enable a market rate to be paid for specific non-core funded programmes and costed into fee structures. Although such practices allow a rapid response to, for instance, changes in demand for specific programmes, they also have the potential to raise issues of equity within an institution, and to lead to an unbundling of roles into separate components such as lecturing, small group teaching, tutoring, examining and assessing, with payment according to the specific tasks that are being undertaken. In some countries, for instance Hong

Kong, there is evidence that some individuals make a career of teaching part-time in a number of institutions on this basis. Their overall pay could exceed that of a full-time appointment in a single higher education institution, although they would be unlikely to be expected to undertake research.

Advantages and challenges of the three approaches, as perceived by senior and middle managers in the LFHE study, are outlined in Table 3.2 (Whitchurch and Gordon 2013).

The *integrated* approach might be said to be align most closely with traditional models of collegial governance, allowing individuals to develop their own niche within a discipline under common conditions and career paths. The *partnership* and *private sector* approaches have gained ground in response to the increasing diversity of institutional missions and activities, providing opportunities for individuals to work and develop their careers in different ways.

It could be argued that institutions that adopt an *integrated* approach give themselves more options and therefore greater flexibility. From the study, the *partnership* model in particular seemed to require ongoing negotiation, which absorbed resources and energy. It was also evident that institutions that were in transition, for instance those seeking to establish a research profile or degree-awarding

Table 3.2 Perceived advantages and challenges of *integrated, partnership* and *private sector* approaches (Whitchurch and Gordon 2013).

	Integrated	Partnership	Private sector
Advantages for institutions	Employment proposition for all academic faculty and staff that is integrated with institutional mission	Allows different employment proposition for segments of the institution to suit different activities	Employment proposition related to market positioning of institution
Advantages for individuals	Sense of community Opportunity to focus on individual strength	Safe environment in which to experiment with new approaches under umbrella of institution	Clear relationship between employment proposition and reward structure
Challenges	Maintaining the employment proposition and market position across a range of activities and staff Development of middle management skills	In employee partnerships, development of management skills In partnership consortia, development of holistic approach across component institutions	Development of middle management skills Development opportunities for staff, including research

powers, were looking for ways of extending the range of employment models available to them, including *private sector* approaches. Others were simply trying to adapt to a rapidly changing environment, or to keep ahead of competitors within that environment. Notwithstanding a less holistic approach to academic activity across the board, the *private sector* model could also include aspects of the *integrated* model, for instance in aligning faculty and professional staff to an institutional employment proposition around competitive advantage. An *integrated* approach also seemed to help to avoid lacunae at middle management level or at the interface between teams. Nevertheless, the other two approaches might usefully be considered by institutions wishing to extend the range of options available to them. Such models enable institutions to make adjustments on an evolutionary basis, although tipping points may occur, such as a new management team, faculty turnover, or internal restructuring, and this is likely to be an ongoing process rather than a one-off event.

The three models can be seen as reflecting different approaches to the employment relationship. It might be said that the *private sector* model creates a transactional relationship, based on defined cost benefits on both sides. The *integrated* model, particularly when the employment proposition is closely related to institutional development and clearly communicated to staff, represents a concerted attempt to achieve recognition of common interests. Success of the *partnership* model can be seen as depending on perceptions about the added value of collaboration between partners by those involved. Where colleagueship develops in the *integrated* and *partnership* models, relationships are made, adjusted and adapted for the purpose in hand. As new approaches are introduced there is likely to be an experimental phase in which they are tried and tested. During this process institutions and individuals weigh the costs and benefits, and if the benefits are not seen to be sufficient, for instance in terms of outcomes or the quality of working lives, this may lead to their discontinuation, whether by design or default. Therefore partnership and collaboration, either internally or with external partners, is likely to involve a more complex discourse, and may present challenges, raising the stakes for managers. As described by one chair of council, they:

> introduce more risk into the situation ... but allow you to achieve things you wouldn't otherwise achieve. (chair of council)

Conclusion

Therefore, rather than focusing solely on structural explanations for organisational gaps and tensions, for instance between formal obligations and informal understandings, between employment and psychological contracts, and between institutional policies and their implementation, the two empirical studies enabled exploration of working relationships as a critical link between policy and practice. Superordinate policy agendas and relationships with policy agencies have led to an awareness of the need for new configurations of people, which may cross structural boundaries but need some co-ordination institutionally. This was the case in an institution that wished to embed employability, the student experience and internationalisation into the curriculum:

> we identified this year that we wanted senior leadership in the field of employability, so we've been out looking for somebody with that skill set, so you are kind of constantly scanning your staffing base and trying to determine what it is that you might need to get a particular focus ... we felt that there were a lot of people doing a lot of things but it wasn't being coordinated and pulled together. (director of human resources)

Institutions therefore seemed to be recognising that there is likely to be a spectrum of staff undertaking a continuum of activity across boundaries. An increasing concern was that individuals should not operate in silos, and that there should be some way of developing synergy across the collective, whether this be at the local, faculty or institutional level:

> The exact balance of activity that the individual does can vary hugely, but that notion of bringing it together is a really critical one ... very different subject areas of course, and very different professional communities and networks. (pro-vice-chancellor, education)

This tension was one that managers appeared to grapple with at all levels and could require an intensive investment of time in one-to-one and local team conversations, being able to take the part of faculty colleagues, playing to individual strengths and circumstances, and steering the collective in ways that would be of optimum benefit for the institution. Thus:

> We need staff who actually will do great research and develop track records ... but will take other people with them, will provide mentoring and support, will work as part of teams and programme and curriculum design, programme leadership. We need people who are really corporate citizens and we can't afford the people who just develop, in quite a selfish way, their own sort of individual career track record. (pro-vice-chancellor, education)

The following two chapters demonstrate how these challenges are being addressed both by rank-and-file faculty and by middle managers.

Chapter 4

Individual responses

Greater uncertainty in higher education environments has led to a significant shift in the positioning of individuals in relation to institutional structures, which can no longer be assumed to offer the security and protection that may have been anticipated when an individual was appointed to a faculty post. There were indications from both studies of a breakdown of the concept of a homogeneous workforce, with entrants from professional practice, media, business and industry at different stages of their careers, having loyalty to practice settings outside higher education, and more individual approaches to their futures. The fragmenting of linear career routes was illustrated by the fact that once within higher education, significant numbers of individuals were departing from their discipline or practice to work on different programmes and/or in different faculties. Furthermore, although rank-and-file respondents in the HEA study were evenly distributed across arts/humanities, social science and science disciplines, only half were teaching and researching in their mainstream 'subject of origin'. People were also prepared to move in and out of higher education to gain relevant experience, and some had a portfolio that involved working part-time in higher education and part-time for another employer:

> So, managing a portfolio of doing ... different pieces of work for different employers, at different points in time. (mid-career, research-only faculty)

There could therefore be significant drift from the original discipline with the result that non-linear career paths were being forged, often arising from professional contacts or emergent interests, in ways that were in themselves considered developmental. In order not to find options closing, individuals could be faced with choices and judgements about, for instance, whether to pursue pure, disciplinary research, applied research that was impact- and commercially-oriented, or research that was more oriented towards the public good. Those later in their careers often attributed any success they had had to the availability of an informal mentor, internal or external to the institution.

Approaches to roles and careers

While some individuals found that policy developments suited their career trajectories, and were able to make use of institutional initiatives, others found their own outlets and were active in pursuing these. Some came to a positive accommodation with institutional provision of professional development, and were proactive in seeking out mechanisms and relationships that would help their career progression; others aligned themselves to formal requirements but hinted at stresses and strains that were not necessarily articulated to colleagues. For instance, applications for promotion were often time-consuming and required considerable thought and effort. If they were not successful, and only minimal feedback given rather than a constructive dialogue being initiated, this could be demotivating, especially where respondents felt that they had few career alternatives. At its most extreme, this could lead to feelings of alienation from the environment that was also a source of identity, creating a barrier to positive relationships.

It was possible to detect three broad approaches to roles and careers, from which a typology was developed, although these were not mutually exclusive and represented a spectrum along which individuals might move according to circumstances.

A reactive approach

This approach represented individuals who appeared to feel constrained by the structures in which they found themselves. Thus a reactive approach could develop when people felt under pressure to meet an expanding range of commitments, for instance teaching and assessment deadlines, applications for research funding and publications, or a contribution to emerging agendas such as employability and public engagement:

> If I looked at everything on my to-do list and wanted to do it to the level that I would like to do it to, I would need twice as much time. So you're constantly saying 'what can I not do ... and what's going to be sacrificed in that?' (mid-career faculty)

Such a response was likely to be fuelled by a sense of having no discretion or control over the amount or type of work, or acknowledgement that this was an issue. Similarly, a lack of clarity about boundaries, or the space an individual was expected to occupy, could lead to feeling that they were expected to be able to do everything in equal measure. Uncertainty about, for instance, which research group an individual might join or which colleagues they might work with meant that they had to depend on seeking colleagues who might 'adopt' them. This type of response covered a spectrum from what might be described as a stoical approach, into which people were locked because of commitments such as family, seeing no alternative, to a stressed reaction involving silent resentment and in some cases ill-health. A stoical response was characterised by a laissez-faire approach to career advancement or even salary, as shown by two respondents in different institutions:

> I don't know about all that stuff [promotions criteria], in truth ... I try to do my job and if I get a promotion I get a promotion or I get a discretionary point, so be it. (mid-career faculty)
>
> You can apply for a discretionary payment, which my mentor recommended that I do this year, but I didn't bother because filling out those forms and having to sell yourself for the sake of, by the time the taxman gets it ... it's not that much money and I'm not motivated by money .... (mid-career faculty)

The first individual went on to suggest that 'it's all politics but anyway, there you go', and was reluctant to enter into micro-politics. A stressed reaction might also involve a desire to leave higher education altogether, as well as a sense of not wanting to show weakness or vulnerability by asking for help, suggesting that such individuals did not believe that they had significant agency to influence their future. Moreover, disillusionment could occur at any level, even when people had worked hard and achieved a promotion:

> I've seen people who have worked incredibly hard to get there and ... after a few years of being in a permanent job, thinking, 'Why did I work so hard for this? This isn't quite what I thought it would be. I assumed I'd go back to having nights and weekends off' and they don't. So I think some people do feel a bit disillusioned. (mid-career faculty)

It was also noticeable that individuals who felt, for whatever reason, isolated from a sympathetic line manager or peer group, were more likely to find it difficult to move out of a reactive positioning. Others had external interests and networks which ameliorated a position of feeling constrained by fixed structures:

> I'm quite lucky that because I move around in several different circles I feel quite well-connected, so don't feel quite as trapped as probably I would .... (mid-career, research-only faculty)

In other cases individuals had made a positive decision, for quality of life and work–life balance reasons, to stay with a job they enjoyed rather than apply for the next rung on the career ladder, although this was not always without some soul-searching:

I do also find it quite difficult that I've chosen not to go for this job and chosen to close what would seem to be climbing up the ladder ... I'm more interested in wellbeing and happiness. (mid-career, teaching-only faculty)

Others found that intrinsic motivation was what drove them:

I'd be happy enough just kind of doing what I'm doing and getting better at it over the years and if that's reflected in getting promotions then that'd be good ... I quite like the level of responsibility of a lecturer ... the level of autonomy and the fewer people that you have responsibility for. (early career faculty)

A pragmatic approach

A pragmatic approach characterised individuals who acknowledged, but also used, the structures in which they found themselves for optimum advantage. This was likely to involve calculating where their effort would be most productive, including adhering closely to the time allocated for each activity in workload models and ensuring that, for instance, the requisite numbers of publications for the Research Evaluation Framework and research grants were achieved in the timeframe. As a number of individuals pointed out, with regret, this 'cost–benefit analysis' could mean devoting less time to the pastoral care of students:

I had to make a decision ... whether I was going to spend two hours with the students or two hours writing a review of their feedback [for the respondent's annual review], and so actually what I did is I just spent two hours with the students because ... the most important thing is to reconnect to them. (mid-career, teaching-only faculty)

However narratives in this category suggested a willingness to enter negotiations with line managers about what adjustments might be made within a workload model over time, and in relation to local agendas:

There are some things that are probably immoveable in some respects, so I couldn't go in and say, 'I want to get rid of some of my teaching', but there's certainly flexibility around saying, 'I want to do this' or 'This is useful to the university' and we'll have a discussion about other, more malleable things ... and particularly because of having a decent research and enterprise income, then that gives you flexibility to say, 'I've brought this in, so let me do some other stuff'. (mid-career faculty)

Other individuals had strong intrinsic motivations in relation to, for instance, helping students, undertaking a specific project, and working with professional or business partners, which brought their own rewards and satisfaction, which some people put above material advancement:

> a mother said to me, 'I firmly believe my daughter wouldn't be alive were it not for you' and that's the most powerful thing I've ever heard, talk about job satisfaction! And that's great because somebody feels that I've enriched their lives in a wonderful way. Career wise? No. No. From colleagues, 'what you do for the school is fabulous, great', but they're not HR, you know, I can't cite any of this! (early career faculty)

As this person indicated, even though local colleagues might appreciate their efforts, these types of activity did not necessarily count in formal criteria for promotion. As well as having intrinsic motivation, such individuals tended to be able to achieve an accommodation with practical issues of, for instance dual careers and family life, accepting a degree of uncertainty, and being open to possibilities:

> I realised that the things I do are inspiring people after me ... I think my main incentive does come from inside, wanting to do what I do more meaning-fully but then also changing the system to be more meaningful. (early career faculty)

Others felt that although institutional structures might not be as facilitative as they would wish, they could try to work round them for the time being. A new regime might change things, for instance the arrival of a supportive line manager:

> I ... very soon realised that ... my skill-set was best served by ... bridging the commercial and academic environment ... the whole area of, 'How can academia and the commercial world co-exist?' ... I like to develop opportunity and where, by its very nature, the academic environment works at a much slower pace than the commercial environment, very often being able to manage that relationship is very powerful for both the academic organisation and the commercial organisation, but we were not encouraged to undertake any of that ... until 12 months ago now ... we have a new Head of Department and it is just a complete breath of fresh air because it is about, if you see an opportunity, go for it .... (late career faculty)

Nevertheless, this person was resigned to the fact that institutional procedures meant that they could not apply for promotion:

> there was a position that came up and I couldn't apply for it because I wasn't at a suitable grade ... so you can meet all the desirable essential criteria in the world but unless you're at a grade in the organisation you're not allowed to apply and it doesn't make sense to me. (late career faculty)

A proactive approach

Individuals in this category were likely to seek out and take opportunities in order to create a distinctive portfolio and develop networks that might be of use in future. As one mid-career member of academic faculty suggested, 'sometimes you might have to bootstrap things yourself'; another said that 'some of it is you going out and getting it'. Examples that were given included community engagement projects, professional or trade body activity, volunteering for institutional committees or working groups, contributing to ATHENA SWAN (the UK's Equality Challenge Unit's Charter for institutions to recognise, progress and commit to equality and diversity in higher education), being an assessor for peers seeking teaching fellowship status, and working with external partners. Being proactive might therefore be seen as a direct response to the multiple and expanding roles adopted by contemporary institutions, particularly with external partners and stakeholders, and increasingly as a pre-requisite:

> the university has changed and there is much more about the bigger picture; you can't just focus … on learning and teaching – that is really important but actually it's bigger and it's about engagement, particularly with industry practitioner type stuff, but the policy stuff is important, and it's worked for me because I feel like I have been supported in what I do, but then that's probably because I did a lot of stuff off my own bat at the start and it's reaped the rewards. (mid-career faculty)

Furthermore, those who felt that they had benefitted, or could benefit, from formal and informal opportunities tended to be those who had sought out what was available, and also sourced contacts and mentors who might support them:

> I think understandably the onus is on the individual to seek out support in the areas that they need, because we are all very different people coming into academic jobs, and need very different things. (early career academic)

Being proactive in developing relationships also appeared to be critical to progressing a career:

> I actually took the effort to speak to our Pro-Vice-Chancellor … and he was the one who actually explained to me about the situation of becoming a reader and becoming a professor and what I would need to put in place … you have to be proactive in finding things out and I think that's good … it's a combination of factors; personal skills like presentation, networking … and somebody who's ambitious and dedicated and wants to search out opportunities … I'm lucky because I'm proactive and because I make an effort to engage with the head of research and the directors here … I've been given these opportunities. (early career, research-only faculty)

It was also important to keep up to date, although some needed encouragement:

> things change so quickly ... and I've had some staff who are just absolutely brilliant with technology and social media and they didn't go on a course, they self taught themselves, they knew it was important ... and they took personal responsibility for making sure they had the skills that they needed to do the job ... Whereas you've other staff members that will wait for a course to be run before they will want to do it. (learning support professional)

Such individuals spoke of identifying imaginative routes towards their goals, following their instincts about what they wanted to do and being prepared to keep options open. They had the confidence to make creative suggestions and appeared to be able to persuade colleagues to back their initiatives, demonstrating added value for the institution or department and finding people who were able and willing to help. This had in many cases paid dividends.

More specifically, they spoke of developing positive relationships with line managers, mentors and peers. Activities such as social networking and attending conferences maximised their opportunities. The following comments typify this approach:

> I proposed to the then head of school that I should take on a dual role, where I continue to teach and introduce a new module ... and then have what started out as an administrative role for ... student experience, which ... evolved and so now ... it's a developmental and strategic role, which the teaching that I do feeds into ... there's push-me-pull-you, so I'll do more hours teaching and then less hours some weeks and then over the summer things will even out. (early career faculty)
>
> I've kind of led the process really myself, I feel. I think someone once called me a 'bit of a hustler', which I was surprised at but I think I look for opportunities within the institution and then dive in ... I did a lot of work with HR [human resources] actually on mental health in the workplace and led initiatives and stuff like that and I just looked for that opportunity ... I just went to see the Head of HR and said, 'Look, this is what I want to do, will you support me?' and they funded me. (late career faculty)

Moreover, there was among these narratives a sense that one opportunity was likely to lead to another, so that success bred success, and such individuals seemed to be able to achieve a steady progression, which made them optimistic about the future. They were prepared to follow their instinct about what they wanted to do and to keep options open, even try to change things. Furthermore, they were aware of the importance of relationships and of fostering these as part of the process of a career on the way to achieving an ultimate ambition:

> I mentioned being a PVC. I don't have to if I don't want to but I could imagine reaching it, and again, I think the skills that I needed and developed during the struggling are exactly what you need because as soon as you get

to certain higher levels, it's all about people and relationships and engaging, and it's not so much about doing experiments. (early career faculty)

Summary

Each category in this typology could be characterised by approaches to work and career, motivations and rewards, and relationships, as summarised in Table 4.1.

Table 4.1 Typology of approaches to work/career, motivations and relationships

Category/ characteristics	Reactive	Pragmatic	Proactive
Approach to work/career	Greater awareness of barriers than opportunities Sense of obligation to complete all tasks to a high level Short-term perspective Low tolerance of uncertainty/ micro-politics	Strategic approach to workload Calculation of benefits/risks of individual activities Willing to negotiate over balance of activity Medium-term perspective Aspirational but may also value work–life balance	Seeks and takes a range of opportunities Aspirational but portfolio approach Views uncertainty with equanimity Medium/long-term perspective Mobile internally and externally
Motivations and rewards	Conscientious completion of every task e.g. 360-degree student care Keeps going Avoidance of failure	Calculation of reward (intrinsic and extrinsic) vis-a-vis task/effort Focus on, for example, teaching or research, if perceived as more rewarding Work–life balance	Intrinsic interest/ rewards Optimistic about potential opportunities Willing to put forward creative ideas/feasibility Keeps options open Confident that career will follow from above
Relationships	Fixed ties to immediate colleagues and student Strict observance of structures Tendency to isolation/ invisibility	Strategic relationships Internal, external and virtual networks Micro-political awareness and skills	Strong and weak ties vertically and laterally Internal, external and virtual networks Open to extended partnership working

In practice individuals are likely to adopt different approaches at different times and in different situations, so that there could be overlaps between being reactive and pragmatic, and between being pragmatic and proactive. The categories therefore indicate characteristic tendencies rather than being tightly boundaried, but represent a broad typology emerging from the studies. From the pragmatic to the proactive end of the spectrum particularly, individuals could be seen to be creating new spaces, activities and contributions that challenged existing practices and expectations, whilst opening up opportunities for themselves and for their institutions.

Those in the pragmatic grouping came closest to putting forward a career plan as such, with milestones and/or timescales, though significant numbers of these also added family commitments and work–life balance into the mix. The reluctance of those in other categories to do so perhaps reflects a degree of uncertainty, and in the case of the reactive group a lack of confidence, and in the proactive group a desire to keep options open and not box themselves in. More generally, this may reflect the fact that early career faculty are unable to make assumptions about what might be achievable and do not see a clear pathway in front of them, possibly because of a lack of understanding of institutional processes. A number of individuals said that it had been a major milestone to achieve a permanent job at all, and that this had taken so much intellectual and emotional effort that they could not contemplate further advancement for the time being. Nevertheless:

> the majority of people now who get permanent academic jobs are confident that they will rise up through the system in the end .... (mid-career faculty)

Variables affecting the different responses, and the ability to achieve a positive accommodation between individual and institution, included the relationships and lines of communication available to the individual, and the malleability of the structures they encountered. There was also some evidence that in institutions with strong histories and cohesive missions (whatever level they might be at in national and international league tables) there was a more effective accommodation between individual and institutional aspirations. This clearly applied at the sub-institutional level, for instance in a business school or health faculty. Much could depend on whether changes were incorporated incrementally when a specific need arose, or whether they were presented as a new departure, for instance the development of a partnership arrangement. Nevertheless individual responses also reflected personal variables such as life and professional experience, confidence levels and motivations.

If a sense of equity is disturbed then a relationship may also become strained, with the result that an individual may put on a public face of acceptance but complain in private and possibly become personally stressed (reactive); accept the perceived inequity but increasingly work around the relationship (pragmatic); argue for a different course of action or try to leave the immediate environment to work with another group or team (proactive). This also comes back to perceptions and the anxieties of individuals about meeting externally imposed targets and standards.

Some individuals appeared to be more relaxed about deriving satisfaction in the job they were doing and finding fulfilment in that. Others were more aware of the playing field they were on and the positioning of others in relation to them. This was likely to be exacerbated in environments where competition was overt and advancement appeared to be a zero sum game (ie there was only space for so many promoted posts, whether or not an individual had fulfilled the criteria).

If these findings are compared with earlier typologies, for instance Dowd and Kaplan's (2005: 709) typology of approaches to careers, the Reactive group might be said to equate roughly with Probationers, who expected their institution to provide a career path for them, the Pragmatic group with Connectors who managed their careers by building networks and seeking social fit, and the Proactive group with Mavericks who focused on 'the academic/market demand for their expertise'. Thus Proactive individuals/Mavericks and Pragmatic individuals/ Connectors had greater confidence in building their own careers, were more comfortable with uncertainty, and saw a greater number of options open to them.

More recently, commentators have noted the 'complex, circuitous and wandering path ... [and] a greater awareness of connections and intersections' (Boon 2010: 4) in relation to careers, particularly in emerging fields such as educational development, in which individuals 'are frequently obliged to negotiate difficult strategic terrain across complex organisational settings' (Land 2010: 14). All these trends point to the need for more discretionary space for adjustments that allow both institutions and individuals to make best use of opportunities. Again this reflects the 'boundaryless career' (Dowd and Kaplan 2005), and it would also seem that there is less expectation of a career for life among younger cohorts, who see themselves as continuously updating their portfolios with a range of activities and projects. It may be for this reason that there was less evidence of Dowd and Kaplan's Conservationists in the HEA study, ie people who become institutional people with strong loyalties to an institution and a 'lockstep' career, leading to a permanent appointment (Finkelstein 2007: 151).

Understandings and interpretations of institutional policies

Across all the categories was some sense of mismatch between formal criteria for promotion, progression and reward, and the reality of who might achieve preference and why. This could be partly due to different interpretations by line managers in different locales in relation to, for instance, the use of faculty discretionary funds or support for attendance at a conference. Policy intentions, therefore, did not necessarily translate seamlessly into the lived reality of individual lives and careers. Furthermore, as shown above, the responses of individuals could differ. Thus the narratives in the studies demonstrated the potential for divergence between policy and practice, and between formal and informal understandings, leading to gaps and dissonances in a number of areas as follows.

Progression and promotion criteria

Long communication lines in institutions that are becoming larger, more complex and often dispersed geographically mean that even where there is detailed documentation about progression and promotion criteria, the practical implications are not necessarily understood. This is exacerbated when new forms of criteria are introduced such as local industry links, work in outreach and the community, or establishment of a high earning master's programme, which were all mentioned by senior managers as a means of broadening opportunities for advancement. Moreover, even when individuals met published criteria, and their line managers agreed that they had met them, extraneous factors such as levels of funding, or the level of competition in a particular year, could mean that promotion was not necessarily forthcoming, or immediately forthcoming. Managing expectations and disappointments, therefore, seemed to be an inherent part of the promotion and progression process.

On the one hand, the following statement from a member of a senior management team was typical in suggesting that because promotion criteria were published, and decisions based on documented evidence, they could be perceived as fair and equitable:

> I think [academic faculty] are astounded because they're sitting maybe observing the outcomes, not knowing what the process is in detail and I think very often they are really surprised at just how clear the consensus is around who meets the criteria and who doesn't meet the criteria and, where there is a disagreement, the discussion around the evidence is done and I think that, for me, gives me confidence in the robustness of the criteria …. (pro-vice-chancellor, education)

On the other hand, there was a strong sense from the narratives that individuals wanted to know, but were not always told, precisely what they needed to do to be promoted, and were frustrated firstly by a lack of detailed feedback, and secondly by having to go through a time-consuming application process several times:

> people always say, 'You are supported, you've got line management, you've got a PDR review.' No. I want to know there are five things I need to do … I want them to say, 'You've got to meet this objective and this objective and this objective. And if you do, then ok. As long as the criteria's not changed, then you're in.' So that would mean a system where you get feedback and then you have conditions … And I don't want to keep re-applying, re-getting the three external references. (mid-career, teaching-only faculty)

However such precise expectations may be unrealistic, and a comment from a director of human resources suggests that work is needed by individuals themselves to internalise what criteria mean, and ways in which they are applied in practice, and that they may need to be proactive in finding this out:

> we did a roadshow the other day for academics around how the promotions work … saying to them, 'Don't just bung your application in cold, find yourself a mentor, talk to your head of department, go and talk … really think it through … go and talk to other people about what they did'. (director of human resources)

The difficulty of defining precisely what promotion criteria might be, and the incorporation of professional judgement about individual contributions, is reflected in the comments of a mid-career member of academic faculty who was a programme director and had achieved a readership:

> I think it's fair to say of any higher education institution, promotion has to run through relatively objective criteria and … some of the things that you can quantify and demonstrate … don't necessarily capture all the things that, you know, reflect a person's full contribution to that institution. (mid-career faculty)

Others who had been successful, for instance in achieving a senior lectureship, spoke directly of having helpful line managers or mentors, and it appeared that informal understandings and knowledge of precedents were invaluable in achieving a promotion. Achieving some kind of profile with members of the promotions panel was also significant. Such opportunities often arose at local level, for instance being a programme leader, or being nominated for a working group, special project or partnership, and could depend on serendipitous conversations. Similarly, discretionary payments for special initiatives could be in the gift of a head of department, and were not necessarily covered by formal institutional policy statements or criteria. Furthermore, one early career, teaching-only faculty on a short-term contract felt that there was a disconnect between institutional and local requirements, and that the system itself was in practice geared to local needs, despite the existence of institutional criteria:

> This year the re-grading process was changed … it was based on the needs of the school … so it's not about what you're doing already, it's about whether or not that could be sustained or needs to be sustained – which was really upsetting because you think, 'Well, I'm doing it, so obviously it needed doing this year but I'm … never going to get any recognition for it!' I've given up asking questions, to be honest, because the answers are just always so smoky. I think the main thing is that a promotion route needs to be opened up, there's got to be some sort of … re-classification of the language that defines the promotion system. (early career, teaching-only faculty)

Significant numbers of respondents referred to the time taken and the stress involved in applying for promotion, especially if they had not been successful. Acknowledgement of their achievements so far and feedback on the reasons for lack of success at a specific point in time were critical to ameliorating a setback and encouraging individuals to keep going and re-apply.

Assumptions about linear careers

From the HEA study there appeared to be systemwide dissonance in approaches to academic roles. Teaching-only roles were found mainly in pre-1992 institutions who were trying to maximise their percentage ratings of research active staff in the Research Evaluation Framework, whereas in post-1992 and post-2004 institutions, where a majority of roles were formally designated teaching and research, many of these were in practice teaching-only. Again this involves implicit assumptions and understandings about what individuals are doing on a day-to-day basis. Moreover the stated value accorded to teaching and teaching development by institutions, even where there were associated career paths leading to a chair, was not necessarily internalised by faculty themselves (Locke, Whitchurch et al 2016). It was also apparent that a significant number of academic faculty feel that they are working in a 'third space' (Whitchurch 2013), with activities such as internationalisation, student welfare, employability and knowledge exchange given as examples of areas with which faculty are expected to engage, in addition to teaching and research agendas.

Of the academic faculty who participated in the HEA study, ie not including members of senior management teams, 30% had entered from careers outside higher education. These included adult and community education, international development, business and industry, the armed services, as well as professional practice, for instance in health and social care. For those later in their careers, dealing with their change in professional identity appeared to be more of an issue than a career track *per se*. A number said that being flexible and willing to take opportunities in new spheres of activity had enabled them to move onwards and upwards. Early and mid-career faculty also seemed sceptical about the reality of a linear career leading straight from a doctorate, recognising that career opportunities could be based on serendipitous meetings and contacts:

> It all sounds rather nepotistic, but there is an element of having been in the right place to meet the right people, doing the right things in order to move and know the next people ... It seems like a standard route but actually it's a very unusual route, being able to come straight the way through various degrees into various jobs into another job into a lectureship .... (early career faculty)

In practice individuals were likely to seize opportunities that came along, sometimes drifting from their disciplinary base and even moving outside teaching, research or knowledge exchange tracks as a result of professional contacts or emergent interests:

> I am a social scientist myself [working in a science faculty], so that's also interesting in terms of the different culture that I have to encounter and the different mentality and different research environment ... and it also reflects other types of changes that are happening in academia and how disciplinary boundaries are blurring right now, so you see a lot of people working in places that you wouldn't expect to see them ... I've worked in a sociology department, in an economics department, in a business school, in a comput-ing school, so I've sort of covered it .... (early career, teaching-only faculty)

Others took on management or leadership roles in relation to, for instance, pedagogic development across their own and adjacent disciplines, sometimes via external networks:

> it got me out of thinking like a biologist and it also gave me an international perspective as well. (mid-career, teaching-only faculty)
> I've always enjoyed mentoring younger women particularly, but mentoring other staff and managing other staff, and I guess setting what I would hope to be a good role model of management in a positive 'bring people with you' way ... I think having come out of the department to link university/ wide was the best thing I could've done, because I learnt so much. I could bring that back to the department ... to lose those links would be a shame. (mid-career faculty)

There were also examples of individuals who had had their time bought out for external activity, for instance with professional or disciplinary bodies:

> I'm not quite a usual member of staff because ... for all of my time really on an academic contract, I've essentially had half of my time bought out on another contract .... (mid-career faculty)

In this way unique and individualised portfolios were being constructed, albeit around a teaching and/or research core, reflecting a 'snakes and ladders' approach (Coates and Goedegebuure 2010), except that these roles were often being undertaken simultaneously. The following illustrates the increasingly lateral reach of some working patterns:

> while I started out as a teaching person, I suppose what success I've achieved has been as much to do with the kind of projects which are on the edge of knowledge exchange really; so ... it's a messy trajectory ... I'm based in an [arts] department but I'm quite an unusual academic inasmuch as I do a lot of work at the medical school ... and I do research projects with local health

charities and that sort of thing ... although I would introduce myself as an 'academic' ... I think I'm ... increasingly happy with the term 'entrepreneur'. (late career faculty)

New relationships are therefore being created all the time, and the following individual, who was formally appointed to a teaching-only role, was extending their activity by seeking out and collaborating with colleagues in order to develop research and scholarship opportunities for themselves:

> I'm trying to engage other colleagues that are more research intensive and use their own expertise and experience in putting a research proposal together ... we are looking into some internal funding for public engagement activities, which also may lead to a research piece .... (early career, teaching-only faculty)

This applied particularly to people who were involved in teaching and learning support and/or academic practice, who might gain experience in contiguous fields before arriving in their ultimate locale. One such person had worked in learning technology and design in an academic department before becoming involved in programme development centrally, and it had been invaluable to have experience at the academic 'coalface':

> it was really valuable to have a foot in both camps and understand ... you could be the middleman for both sides, which was quite useful. (mid-career, academic developer)

Another individual who had worked in careers, and was now focusing on employability, described how it was important to have a teaching qualification and links with academic colleagues:

> we're not a support service, we're actually there right in the learning and teaching space, and I think that has been a big, big driver of me, for me, within this role and this institution .... (mid-career, learning support professional)

At the same time there is dissonance in the fact that it is increasingly common for institutions to develop career tracks with a specific focus, including learning and teaching, the student experience, professional practice, and knowledge transfer. However, even where institutions were making it a priority to both develop and publicise career pathways, these were generally based around assumptions of a linear career, possibly with linked sideways moves, as in Strike's 'career climbing frame' (Strike 2010). The following quotation demonstrates how individuals starting from the same disciplinary point might over a 20-year period splinter and spread across into what this person terms 'sub-careers', so that academic identities develop both temporally and spatially to become multi-track and heterogeneous:

So the cohort of people like myself ... who ... went through PhDs at just slightly different times in the same institution ... and so it's that network of mates who are also not direct colleagues, in that most of them are in ... individual sub-careers in slightly different directions or different places ... become both the sounding board and I guess to a certain degree, the point of reflection where you look at how their careers have moved and yours have moved ... There is a range of different places where we've got insights into what being an academic means, in different set ups as well ... and it's nice that is spread across different institutions, different academic systems. (mid-career faculty)

It was repeatedly noted in the narratives that contacts and networks were important for providing external references and that meeting the stated criteria for each point on a career ladder was unlikely to be sufficient on its own. This non-linear process could also have a double edge in that it could involve activity outwith a prescribed workload model:

You have to be more externally focused [for a readership or chair] ... But how do I gain my external focus? ... I'm on the board of a professional body ... I teach at [a Russell Group] University and I'm an external examiner at two institutions, so this is where I gain my reach. But ... my external stuff probably takes a month of my time. And if I said to my line manager, and I was open, 'Is it ok ...', they might say, 'Oh, that's going to distract him in our time'. But the criteria are crying out for me to have external links, but how can I get them? (mid-career, teaching-only faculty)

Furthermore, individuals did not always appreciate that for a promoted post there might be some additional work needed, for instance in relation to local team management and leadership, and that this could be developed along the way although it might not be made explicit.

To some extent these discontinuities were recognised by senior managers and again it was a question of changing the perceptions of individuals as to how roles that might be seen as a pre-requisite for the next step in a career might be interpreted and 'pushed' to their full potential:

there were many staff who weren't absolutely clear ... of what the criteria are and also I think, importantly, how to fulfil the criteria; sometimes staff will say, 'If I become a programme leader, that's administration', whereas you need to turn that around and say, 'But actually you can now lead and drive forward some innovations across a set of modules, and that starts to give you that leadership awareness which will help'. (pro-vice-chancellor, learning and teaching)

Conversely there was evidence in both the LFHE and HEA studies of staff in learning support or staff development roles undertaking academic activity, including lecturing, student mentoring, marking and assessment. Some were paid on an hourly rate, and others incorporated this within their existing role, reinforcing the fact that career tracks for professional and academic roles are no longer clear-cut (some learning support and development appointments are made on academic contracts, and others on professional contracts of employment). Frustrations of a mismatch between systems and processes and day-to-day reality were reflected in statements such as:

> It's difficult not having a place within our job families where you can say, 'Well I've got an expertise but it happens to be 50% here and 50% there', and there's no middle place to put it. (mid-career, academic developer)

The value accorded to teaching

On the one hand, there appeared to be a widespread policy intention on the part of institutions to raise the status of teaching, so that it was valued equally with research for the purposes of progression and promotion:

> [we need to] better align the nature of the work that people are doing, the work that the institution needs them to do to the contracts that they are on and then ensure, within those pathways, that their promotion and advancement prospects are no less disadvantageous than those who choose to go on other routes ... if staff have not the capability or the ambition to be research active in a REF-able sense ... then we have to have a conversation about, 'How can they maximise and optimise their contribution to the university, get job satisfaction from that, see a clear trajectory for themselves, and play to their strengths?' (pro-vice-chancellor, education)

On the other hand, there was a strong perception among faculty that achievements in research had more purchase than those in teaching for the purposes of promotion, despite policy statements to the contrary:

> The kind of press releases that accompanied ... [promotions to chairs] said that they were purely on the basis of their teaching excellence ... Well [they were] not purely, because they were also engaged in research .... (mid-career, teaching-focused faculty)

Some people on teaching-only contracts therefore felt disadvantaged, even where they felt that their contribution was of significant value:

> the contribution that I make has changed the culture of the school ... and I know that it's been instrumental in making so many important vital

changes ... I'm using my academic insight and knowledge to perform these roles, so really there should be an academic contract, it shouldn't just be teaching [only] ... because ... that's a dead-end and where's the progression? (early career, teaching-only faculty)

As a result, significant numbers of faculty having teaching-only and also 'teaching-focused' teaching and research contracts confessed to undertaking research 'on the side', not only to maintain their skills and knowledge in their disciplinary field, but also to keep their options open for future applications for promotion. Conversely, some of those in posts with a formal teaching and research remit had effectively become 'teaching-only', although not designated as such, and preferred to focus in this way. This situation might be with or without the tacit knowledge and agreement of their line manager and institution and, in practice, much might depend on local managers:

it's quite noticeable that when you get someone like a new dean who is more research focused, then suddenly research jumps up the priority list, whereas if somebody comes in who has been brought in to deliver the teaching more efficiently, then research doesn't get a look in. So that very much comes down to the personalities of the individuals involved. (research-only faculty)

Interestingly, although this person had a research-only contract, they felt that not being involved in teaching disadvantaged them:

My feeling is that unless you're involved in teaching, you are almost over-looked within the university. (research-only faculty)

It would therefore seem that there are often implicit understandings about the value accorded to teaching and research, depending on local contexts, whatever formal statements are made. The following statement from a professor who had been promoted on the basis of their teaching illustrates the weight and influence of perceptions, whether justified or not:

I think there still are fault lines which, even when institutions are committed to healing those fault lines, exist between research and teaching ... I know there are here and it's not necessarily that people are thinking, 'research is more important than teaching' (or vice versa even), it's kind of a cultural thing ... the reason for mentioning it is that that cultural kind of mindset can have implications [for the perceptions of early career faculty]. (late career faculty)

Others saw the introduction of teaching-only pathways as providing greater clarity about what steps were required to progress, with for instance newly introduced knowledge transfer or academic enterprise pathways appearing to be more difficult to understand or navigate. However, although a specified career track could give people a planning horizon, it did not necessarily open up opportunities.

Thus, although higher education institutions may state in their formal criteria that there is parity between teaching and research for promotion and progress, the general perception persists that greater weight is likely to be accorded to research, and that higher levels of excellence would be required to be promoted on the basis of teaching:

> I think sometimes ... when people move and progress in their careers, they can be superb researchers, useless teachers, and get promoted, and ... it's a bit concerning at times. I'm not saying everyone should be brilliant at everything, but I think there should be parity in that. So sometimes I have felt, for someone on an education-only contract, I have to meet all the criteria whereas you can be a top-notch researcher and rubbish at your teaching or admin and still get on, and I think that's a little bit unfair .... (mid-career faculty)

This corroborates evidence in the literature that 'higher level criteria [for readers and professors] prove more transparent and less controversial to measure', external evidence making them 'more visible and easier to validate ... [whereas] [d]ebates of how to measure excellence in the more private arena of classroom performance create the most controversy' (Parker 2008: 249–250).

Thus, although in the minority numerically at less than 50% in the UK, those with teaching and research responsibilities continue to be regarded as having primacy as the core of the institutional workforce, again illustrating the dissonance between stated policy and implicit understandings. This situation is likely to particularly disadvantage those entering higher education from practice settings:

> a weak informal research culture ... undermine[s] the formal discourse about the desirability of research activity ... [with] stark mismatches of values between the previous practice context and that of the university. (Gourlay and Sabri 2010: 2)

Changing perceptions about the value accorded to teaching and research, therefore, which were often dependent on day-to-day understandings between local managers and faculty, appeared to be a critical task for institutions.

Workload models

Workload models were constructed at institutional, faculty or departmental level, with differing degrees of flexibility, and were also subject to interpretation by line managers. There was, within the framework of formal job descriptions and workload allocation models, a keen awareness by individuals that while such models aimed to achieve transparency and equity, they did not necessarily reflect the reality of day-to-day working, for instance the pastoral care of students, within the time allocated for teaching. Nor did they account particularly well for interdisciplinary and external partnership working:

> we have a departmental workload model … but it's patently inadequate for people like me, for most people it's okay but for almost everybody there are gaps in it, but for anybody who's trying to work across faculties and departments and work in new ways, it's difficult. (late career faculty)

Similarly, administration tended to be invisible and not to be incorporated appropriately, particularly for those with programme or team leader responsibilities:

> the administration for my role isn't captured very well in that form at all. So it might say 120 hours admin for the year as a subject leader and you can do that in the first term *easily* … you could do that in the short third term. So the real difficulty that I've found is that because the administration isn't reflected in the workload effectively, what suffers is the research. (mid-career faculty)

Others suggested that, when apportionment of load was calculated, this was likely to be based on what a head of school referred to as 'notional splits'. Furthermore, time sheets, which were completed by rule-of-thumb or even guesswork, were not an accurate reflection of actual time spent:

> It's a time management survey, and everybody makes it up. You make it up when you get the tenth email reminder to 'do it now' because you've missed all the deadlines … So I think it is kind of guesswork and it's quite interesting about us collectively that we don't really know. (mid-career faculty)

Perhaps more significantly however, it was pointed out that workload models can become a straightjacket, inculcate what one head of department described as a 'work to rule' mindset, and reduce any opportunities for understandings to develop through informal contacts and conversations:

> there's a danger and a culture of kind of accounting for one's time, which can erode collegiality. A lot of that depends on the skills of the individual line manager and also on the atmosphere of collegiality that exists within a school, so whether those people are speaking to each other … because we are all under intense time pressure, some of that corridor conversation, some of the informal lunches, the catching people afterwards for a pint … a lot of that has been eroded over the last 10 or 15 years … And what it means

is that people therefore tend to work more to the book and they miss that opportunity for informal arrangements. (late career faculty)

At their most successful, workload models are likely to 'play to people's skill sets, allowing them to focus in a way that they accept and welcome' (head of administration). In particular, adjustment may be required in practice by local managers to take account of, for instance, extended hours and 'thinking time', even if this cannot be made explicit. This tended to be easier in smaller departments where individuals knew local circumstances such as which programmes and activities took more time, and where there were implicit understandings about compensating mechanisms.

Provision of professional development

Contemporary institutions are likely to have extensive programmes of formal provision including, for instance, training for teaching, leadership and management, research methods and writing for publication. Most UK institutions require those without a formal teaching qualification to undertake this as part of their probationary period. A number of institutions in the studies had formal mentoring schemes and arrangements for peer review. However, there was a widespread view among faculty interviewed that training programmes were less developmental than individually-tailored, just-in-time initiatives such as peer feedback, mentoring and networking, the latter including reflective dialogue via social media, especially among early career faculty. This is likely to be a reflection of time pressures on individuals and a feeling that activities have to be prioritised in order to meet deadlines. It also illustrates the tension for individuals between wanting training, but finding that it can become another pressure rather than a support:

> there are all sorts of contradictions here, aren't there? ... I guess one of the obvious things would be to provide more training, but when you take on [a management] role you don't feel you've got the time to take on [formal training] ... then the training itself becomes an additional burden ... how do you balance that? (mid-career faculty)

This person therefore preferred just-in-time support that also provided a space for reflection and exchange of experience about what might and might not work in specific situations. Thus, experiential development is often seen as more valuable than formal interventions. Such support could be both local and available across a broader inter-institutional network:

> There are problems in the role that I was facing on day one, challenges that I'm dealing with kind of very much on an unfolding basis, and it's like, 'Okay', and stopping and thinking about those and having the opportunity

to talk to other people in similar roles at close quarters ... I guess partly the reason ... that I haven't felt particularly I need to seek specific institution support has been ... [I've] got many mates who are also in the business and therefore we can talk openly with them about this and they can to us, and so in that sense there's a lot of informal support, or at least points of reflection, which is useful in keeping you sane. (mid-career faculty)

At the formal and institutional level, the responsibility for developmental activity could also be split in different ways, for instance between human resources departments for topics such as management, leadership, appraisal and mentoring, and academic practice/teaching and learning units for all aspects of pedagogic practice and research skills. However, decisions about who should participate and who might benefit is likely to be the responsibility of a local line manager such as a head of department, with 'just-in-time' assistance given by peers, colleagues and mentors on a day-to-day basis. Joining up this activity laterally (across human resources and academic practice units for instance) and vertically, from such units to local managers, faculty and professional staff, communicating what is available and what the outcomes might be, is likely to be a more complex matter than simply having formal provision in place.

Conclusion

The diversification of the workforce, of contractual models, and of career paths has put more onus on the individual in developing a portfolio of activity that will distinguish them in building a future in higher education. Possible responses to less certain contexts may be characterised along a *reactive, pragmatic* and *proactive* continuum, according to individual circumstances and career positioning. At the same time there is increased potential for the way that institutional policies are perceived and interpreted locally, leading to possible dissonance around key areas such as progression and promotion criteria, assumptions about linear careers, the value accorded to teaching, workload models, and the provision of professional development. This has led to a critical role for local managers in optimising the contribution of individuals to school, departmental and institutional objectives, which are themselves diversifying. This role will be explored in the following chapter.

Chapter 5

The role of middle managers

Whatever employment models are adopted, the way that they are interpreted is likely to be critical. The studies suggest that the psychological contract is becoming a more organic relationship in which middle managers, such as heads of school or department and programme leaders, are increasingly creative in responding to a variety of individual circumstances. This reflects the fact that in contemporary institutions, which are complex and often dispersed, it is not simply a question of senior management teams defining policies and local managers implementing them. As one director of human resources put it, '[w]orkable solutions occur largely case-by-case'. This is less likely to involve providing orderly one-off solutions within a finite timescale than working on an ongoing basis in an exploratory way to seek a common basis for working arrangements. Although people management is now recognised as a strategic function and included in institutional governance processes, in many cases it is increasingly devolved to schools and departments. Moreover this is often seen by middle managers as more challenging than managing budgets, although there tends to be more training and support for the latter. In distributed management arrangements, therefore, managing people is no longer something undertaken by a minority of managers at the most senior levels, but starts at the level of the programme and project team.

Local managers can be instrumental in how moves towards greater flexibility are presented and perceived. There is an emerging literature on their roles (including, for instance, Clegg and McAuley 2005; Kallenberg 2007; Meek et al 2010), which are not always fully understood or recognised by institutions. Flexibility may be provided by custom and practice as much as by formal provision, and a key responsibility for such managers, therefore, is likely to be in assessing the point at which local arrangements might be optimal. This might include, for instance, the development of teams that can teach across a range of programmes in ways that can be adjusted if necessary year-on-year, and the use of flexitime to accommodate the balance of activity at departmental as well as at individual levels. More recent studies point to what is sometimes a difficult positioning between senior management teams and rank-and-file faculty, the balancing act that middle managers may have to undertake, and the need for support for these managers (Pepper and Giles 2015; Floyd 2016; Davis et al 2016).

Although it has been suggested that there is a need for 'leaders and managers who personalise the workplace' (Blass, Jasman and Shelley 2010: 35), they often have little support for their roles:

> the lack of leadership education for mid-level managers, along with the terms and conditions governing their appointment are major weaknesses in many university systems .... (Knight, Baume et al 2007: 434)

This point was echoed by Hall (2009), who suggests that:

> a high proportion of relatively inexperienced academics will be responsible for directing teams of researchers, technicians and others, yet these 'managers' are often ill prepared for the task. (p. 8)

One reason for this may be that communication of human resource strategies 'to those managers who have to implement related policies and practices ... is rather left to chance' (Guest and Clinton 2007: 42). This chapter will explore how such managers provide a critical link between institutional structures and policy implementation in practice, and ways in which institutions might support them effectively in order to ensure that they also feel part of the collective steer of the institution.

The influence of middle managers

In large and complex institutions, the impact of policy decisions is likely to be played out in local settings such as schools and departments, and responsibility for outcomes to devolve onto middle managers:

> the policy does tend to be, because of the unitary nature of the institution, at [senior management team] level, but the implementation ... can be devolved to faculties, and faculties can take slightly different views, depending on their traditions and where they see their objectives. (pro-vice-chancellor, education)

From the studies it was clear that the influence of such managers could be critical for rank-and-file faculty on initial entry to higher education, in relation to subsequent career moves, and in day-to-day working:

> a change of management can suddenly change everything ... and the culture in the faculty changed almost overnight with the new person .... (late career faculty)
>
> whatever your contract says ... your immediate line manager is absolutely critical to what you do .... (late career faculty)

The positive aspects of this were reflected, for instance, in a local manager's agreement to adjust the balance of activity over time in ways that met both individual and institutional goals:

> Xxx is just wonderful to work with ... because she'll say, '... you don't need to do a lot over the summer ... but also why don't you do some research, why don't you do some papers ... Let's block out the time in order to see what we can do' ... and so I have a very flexible and a very open set of colleagues who are rooting for me essentially, they see the potential and they say, 'if you want to research for two months, just go away and do it, as long as x, y and z are completed by September' ... So I have a very, very, very, happily flexible ... but then again, in terms of the actual contract, it doesn't *quite* say that at this point in time. (early career faculty)

In such cases middle managers were maintaining the spirit of institutional requirements on the basis of implicit understandings that did not necessarily reflect, for instance, precise time allocations for specific activities in a workload model.

Another member of faculty with caring responsibilities, who worked part-time and found it difficult to incorporate all the activities that they needed to be eligible for a promotion, or to develop networks external to the institution, described how their line manager was able to be flexible within a workload model by looking for opportunities for them to undertake supervision and marking, as these tended to be less time-consuming but would count towards the necessary hourly target in the model. This shows how a line manager could be instrumental in providing discretionary time and space that was facilitative to an individual, and also 'protected' space (Leisyte 2016) in which an individual can grow their career according to their academic strengths and interests. This could also involve boundary crossing and a flexing of academic and organisational priorities (Henkel 2016). Thus another middle manager, by offering 'protection' from institutional 'bureaucracy', allowed the following individual to focus on building partnerships with industry:

> the dean came to me one day and said, 'I'd like you to head up this new facility', which was very empowering ... and after a while I said to him, 'Look, I'm not used to bureaucracy ... but I realise it's a necessity in this environment', he said, 'Leave the politics to me, you just deal with what you think are the commercial realities of what needs to be done' and the working relationship was brilliant and the opportunity to be that catalyst between [the university and industrial partners] .... (mid-career faculty)

Furthermore, a line manager could be absolutely critical to the renewal of a contract:

> if your line manager leaves or if you're coming up for the end of your contract, you have to rely on the fact that your line manager is going to fight

your corner and they're going to make sure your contract is renewed because you can't rely on the fact that some other director in this department will support what you're doing. (early career, research-only faculty)

They could also be instrumental in recommending discretionary points and promotions, local titles for faculty roles and responsibilities such as the student experience or internationalisation, as well as funding for conferences and study leave. There was evidence that discretionary payments in particular can be much appreciated by, and provide an incentive to, those who receive them:

> I've had lots of success with discretionary increments in the past and there are kind of bonus awards as well ... I've been able to develop outside of my normal role or with colleagues we've developed something together ... So it's very dependent on your line manager as to how your promotion is helped along. (mid-career, academic developer)
> to my delight and complete astonishment, my line manager at the time secured to me a £1,000 bonus which I didn't know was happening, a one-off kind of thing, just because she made a case to the college that I was working particularly hard at something. So I've now sort of written references for colleagues to do similar things and I think that is actually quite a good thing, partly because it can be handled very locally .... (mid-career faculty)

Such initiatives could involve fine judgements about performance and potential, some of which might be clearly documented in relation to, for instance, publications and student feedback. Other aspects might be more speculative as to whether, for instance, study leave might lead to a major publication or research grant, or involve working with key individuals in another institution. The experience of individual line managers is likely to come into play here, for instance knowledge about precedents within and outside the school or department.

They may also be influential in promoting the careers of increasing numbers of individuals who do not see themselves on a linear career trajectory, or are working in new fields and/or pursuing new agendas:

> there's plenty of provision for flexible working ... so there's all sorts of support for career routes that aren't purely focused on nothing but work and promotion ... I guess I feel like the options are all there but that underlying all that is a desire to support people to achieve and grow as best they can and as best they want to. (early career faculty)

One academic developer described a tension around, for instance, how far they should be involved in research into practice, applications for project funding, and authoring publications, and the role that local managers would have in this:

> The research side is entirely optional, depending on the different managers I've had over the time, that's either been not allowed or encouraged. And so

much of the research I do is outside of the 9 to 5, and it's all related to the job and it all feeds back in, but yes, that's something I do kind of on the side. (mid-career, academic developer)

Issues of equity

Nevertheless, local managers' hands may also be tied by structural mechanisms at institutional level designed to maintain perceptions of equity across the board, for instance in relation to discretionary increments:

> We don't have scales with what used to be called bonus points on the top, because they're very dangerous from an equality point of view ... because they can cause all sorts of problems with equal pay ... And the unions very much welcomed that because it was perceived that only the 'chosen few' got into these extra points at the top. And then there was always a danger that someone ... could compare themselves to someone on this 'extra' and say, 'Well, what's the difference between me and them in terms of what I'm doing?' (director of human resources)

In this type of context therefore there was also the possibility that the influence of local managers could be perceived as disproportionate:

> I guess something you learn over time is that the person who often gets put forward to do something is someone who, for whatever reason, has recently come to the attention of a manager ... I've been on some bigger grants but only as a co-investigator, and that's an area where I think I'd have got much more research done and taken my research to a much higher level if I'd have cottoned on to what was happening rather quicker. (late career faculty)

Although this individual was sanguine about establishing a profile, there was the potential for discontent if individuals felt that they had not been dealt with fairly. This in turn could be very localised:

> while I'm grateful to the institution for how it's helped me grow and develop as a person and as an academic, there are also corners of the institution which are quite toxic. I mean, certain individuals who build power bases and king-doms and I just try and avoid them .... (late career faculty)

This in turn could lead to different career chances and outcomes in adjacent departments:

> you can see that even with the same faculty, you belong to the different departments, you have a different culture, you have different support, then you become different people. (early career faculty)

Furthermore the disproportionate effect of a negative relationship with a line manager is clearly expressed in the following comment:

> I think it's *people* that can either help or hinder, largely (whether that's colleagues or line managers or anybody really) and that's pretty much the same throughout life, isn't it? ... Unfortunately, if you don't get on with people, that can be a big obstacle. It's more of an obstacle than the advantage of having a good working relationship with somebody being a positive because it can actually not prevent you from doing your job but it makes things extremely awkward. (mid-career faculty)

Even where relationships were deemed to be reasonable, a purely formal, by-the-book implementation of policy could, at worst, lead to a loss of opportunity for individuals to develop potentials that might not be precisely legislated for, be it in workload models, promotion criteria, or development opportunities.

Managing performance

Local managers often trod a narrow path, and the issue of managing peers on what might be a temporary basis, for instance in relation to reviewing performance, was raised on a number of occasions as an area in which they required support:

> you've got to have difficult conversations and you've got to have a proper process ... I know it's a complex discussion but I envisage that I'm going to have to have conversations around, 'are [individuals] moved to teaching and scholarship? Do we come to some kind of enhancement package?' ... I think I do need some help on that. (mid-career faculty, middle manager)

Such conversations were inevitably around enabling a convergence of institutional and individual interests. One senior manager made the link between professional development and performance management, and the role of middle managers in achieving an approach that was enhancing for individuals and addressed their aspirations, but was also linked with institutional requirements, noting that this process, if not sensitively handled, could be stressful for both managers and faculty alike:

> we have [performance management] policies but ... you would lose the will to live by the time they would become effective, and I think line managers, particularly at the head of school level, middle managers, find them extremely stressful ... as I see it, there's an armoury of things, of policies and incentivisation and things like that .... (pro-vice-chancellor, education)

A number of respondents saw this as requiring a culture change, in which professional development was likely to depend on an openness to regular feedback:

> There's a reluctance of people to see [performance management] as a legitimate thing to get feedback and there's a reluctance to give feedback, whether it's praise or confronting areas where improvements are needed. (director of human resources)

Changing cultures therefore involved a bringing together of top down and bottom up understandings:

> I'm trying to get across a view that feedback on your performance is an entitlement, not something that is done to you. But that's a culture shift, that's not here at the moment ... you're going to have to have a greater level of trust in the organisation ... there's generally buy-in to the direction of the strategy but worry about what it means for me as an individual. (director of human resources)

In turn, at its most effective, performance review was likely to be an ongoing and dialogic process. When it can be internalised in a developmental way, it therefore has the potential to become:

> something that you [do] in order to provide yourself with evidence about your excellence or lack of excellence as a teacher ... these are tools you actually need to understand your own performance and to improve it ... [we have to] engage people with the possibilities of enhancement because they're so profound. I think you are transformed by the modelling that you receive. (academic developer)

Regular conversations also enabled a balanced view to be taken of what might not have gone so well. As part of this process, pre-empting problems was also seen as a significant aspect of being a manager:

> very often people don't ... realise there is a problem or they recognise there is a problem but they don't know what to do about it ... In very many cases [appointing a research adviser] has been extremely effective ... in moving people back into the right space again. (head of school)

This type of steer was realistic in recognising that challenges might occur, but had been successful in cutting through perceived difficulties before they became entrenched, guiding younger researchers and helping to overcome a drop off in research activity at certain points in their careers.

A culture of feedback

One head of administration spoke of developing a 'culture of feedback', saying that this should be part of managers' everyday activities. This feedback was particularly valuable in relation to promotion, especially when an individual had been knocked back and felt discouraged:

> the formal process of ... promotion ... It feels like quite an alienating thing, and I had had experience of being kicked back, I was refused promotion once before getting it. (mid-career faculty)
> within the School ... [people] were actually really supportive and helpful in giving me feedback. So somebody who is quite senior ... met with me ... and kind of told me what I needed to do to get promoted ... so they were really, really supportive and helpful. (mid-career faculty)

Others stressed the value of establishing an 'ongoing conversation' as opposed to a single, one-off annual review, illustrating the perceived importance of meaningful, day-to-day interactions, leading to more nuanced understandings of a range of local factors which might affect career decisions:

> But what the paper says and what the reality is, is never the same, but it also differs from year to year, so if I feel that next year, for instance, I'm drowning with teaching or admin, I feel that I have the right to go to my Head of School and tell them, 'Listen, this year I've died, can I take one less module next year, please ...?' or, for example, 'If I find a research opportunity with some colleagues, can I pursue that for a while, will you give me that?' and usually you have the room to negotiate such things with your Head of School and accommodate everybody's needs and things like that (early career faculty).

Some respondents also referred to staff surveys as a way of gauging perceptions more generally, as well as the use of blogs for ongoing communication. These could lead into and stimulate two-way conversations and set the agenda for regular 'town' meetings. However if the feedback from surveys was not perceived to be taken on board, cynicism could set in and negate the purpose, therefore it was important that concerns that were raised were acknowledged and acted upon, or at least that some kind of discussion took place. Thus, one middle manager responsible for international partnerships spoke of an 'open office policy' whereby anyone could call a meeting, either one-to-one or involving a group. This manager didn't want structures to get in the way of communication, and success was regarded as success for the team.

Another head of department described how individuals might be accommodated in ways that played to their strengths and motivations:

> I don't think it's an exact science ... As we move to a more marketised, competitive and differentiated higher education sector, what we try and do ...

within the finance model, is to give people a little bit of space, so that if something comes along there's some space for them to do things. (head of department)

This not only involved a certain amount of creativity, but also the capacity to hold in suspense precise structural frameworks and timescales if necessary, without appearing to contravene them. This might be described as having the confidence to maintain space (and associated resource) that is permanently 'pending', not yet precisely accounted for, and to be filled with activities not yet clearly articulated. An example might be giving an individual time to work on a one-off research or consultancy project, and finding some resource to cover their teaching for this period. This type of discretionary space can be offered by heads of school and department to provide opportunities whilst maintaining day-to-day practices and relationships.

Although the relationship of rank-and-file faculty with line managers inevitably has dimensions of power and authority, with this loaded formally towards the manager, individuals who were able to achieve what might be termed 'mature' relationships acknowledged that communication was a two-way street, and made it their responsibility to keep senior colleagues informed about their activities:

> I'm very aware that other key people are informed of what I'm doing because then it connects up other things they're doing – so I don't want to do stuff completely rogue ... So I'm very clear about speaking to people within the central management and senior people, so they know what I'm doing, so actually we can join stuff up now and again and then that means the vice-chancellor knows what I'm doing, so it's kind of useful in that sense. (mid-career faculty)

It was also evident that flatter management structures and a spread of expertise about institutional agendas across academic departments had facilitated a shift to more dialogic ways of working:

> my line manager is also in my team, so depending on what conversation we're having, I might be telling him what to do or he might be telling me what to do, depending on whether it's something he's doing as a lecturer working for a subject leader or whether it's something I'm doing and reporting to a line manager. (mid-career faculty)
> It's a very flat hierarchy, it's quite a porous hierarchy as well and it's a 'can do' place ... if you've got an idea, people won't just dismiss you, you really can do things and it's always been like that ... if you've got an idea, people will coalesce around it and will support you. (mid-career faculty)

Therefore creating manageable units, in which a line manager could have an overview of the faculty for whom they were responsible, and interact meaningfully with individuals, would also appear to be critical:

I think the support of the Head of Department, particularly within a department like mine which is small, that's very helpful ... It's very easy for someone who is supposedly overseeing what everyone's doing, to not actually know what everyone is doing, and within that sort of circumstance it's very easy for certain people to carry more of the load than others and I think at the moment our head of department, and our previous head as well, both had a very strong oversight of what was going on and a desire to balance and equate and just make sure everything works at a sort of level, which as an early career person is quite useful .... (early career faculty)

A critical link

The role of middle managers as a critical link between individuals and the institution was a strong thread in the narratives, both from the point of view of individuals and their managers. Local loyalties to schools and departments could be more supportive and motivating than institutional loyalties, especially in large institutions where senior management teams might seem quite distant:

there has been in the last few years a very strong 'them and us' theme, when 'they' are the [university] and we are the school of xxx, and we tend to feel that the senior management ... act in a rather draconian way ... the vast majority of people in the school wanted us to enter everyone in the school for the research evaluation framework ... it was very important that we felt that we had ownership of that ... that was enormously important to our sense of wellbeing. (school director of research)

Despite their in-between positioning, a significant number of respondents noted the value of middle managers as providing local and interpretive relationships to counteract what were seen as the relationship with a collective institutional 'management', reflected in policy documents. This was particularly important in providing individual feedback and recognition that might not be forthcoming through formal channels:

I've secured two really large EU projects ... I never felt like I've had any recognition for having done that ... I know it's not like the private sector, where you get a bonus for doing something but I don't even get like a verbal pat on the back for doing it, which wouldn't cost them anything! ... I think they worry that then they're creating an argument for people to ask for more money or ask for more holiday or ask for rewards, which they don't want to give to people. (early career, research-only faculty)

From a middle manager's point of view, however, this positioning could also lead to feeling squeezed between the senior management team and the school:

> I was director of research for the Research Evaluation Exercise (REF) for the school ... and I really disliked being part of that ... I suppose part of it was that I was given power and responsibility to make certain decisions, that actually there was a head of school above me and then there was a huge hierarchy of people who were preparing for the REF (which is understandable at the [university] level) but I sort of felt that I was sandwiched between colleagues and I wasn't really in control of the strategy and the process. (faculty director of research)

Middle managers therefore could have a difficult path to navigate between the integration of institutional policy with policy in practice, undertaking an interpretive and transformational function, and bridging gaps that may have opened up, at the same time as being accessible to those on the ground.

Some senior respondents emphasised the ability to take academic leadership roles as a pre-requisite for a promoted post, reflecting the fact that leadership capability has become a component of progression in a career track. Although this has not necessarily been acknowledged explicitly by institutions in the past, there were signs of an emerging awareness of this role by both institutions and individuals:

> when we bring in academics and we appoint them, we appoint them on their subject knowledge and possibly some teaching experience ... then pretty much our academics end up managing a module ... managing people, they matrix manage people maybe older than them, more experienced than them and it always strikes me that they come in thinking it's going to be one type of role, which is being excellent at their subject and be able to articulate that well ... but actually there's a large part of leadership and management which starts very, very early on. (pro-vice-chancellor, education)

Increasingly, as roles become more complex and multi-faceted, it is not uncommon for individuals to report to more than one manager for different aspects of their work, in relation to, for instance, teaching, research, knowledge exchange, agendas such as employability, and even work on an overseas campus. This was exemplified in a large profit-making school that employed their own educational development team, who not only worked with the head of teaching in the school but also across the institution and with students:

> I have a very key relationship with the director of education at the ... school, and ... with all the main stakeholders that contribute to what my role is trying to achieve ... So I have big links with learning and development, with talent development ... with the international [office], with student support .... (educational developer)

The potential fluidity of such arrangements, and ways in which individuals draw on a range of relationships according to need, is further illustrated by the following:

> the line manager is really the head of school, but then we have, I mean, you have the director of research and director of education and I have a mentor as well, and then for my admin role there's the deputy head of school .... (mid-career faculty)
> the head of our research team ... although she's not my line manager, she's sort of another boss if you like ... Although it's a slightly strange relationship because she doesn't really have any kind of formal management role ... in some ways I treat her a bit more like a manager ... And I have a mentor as well. (early career faculty)

Theoretically the overarching line manager such as a head of department or school should maintain an overview. However there is also potential for individuals to agree different work packages with different managers, and even for line managers to be played off against each other, illustrating the complex roles that middle managers have in practice, and the potential for lacunae in communication.

Thus, achieving relationships that were facilitative but also provided a framework for and feedback on activity appeared to be welcomed by individuals, but were a delicate balance, and also required an investment of time by local managers:

> I've been lucky ... my managers ... are very light-touch, in fact they're too light-touch, I would say. So my criticism there would be, I would have liked a bit more management and it's not even management, it's just a check in to say, 'What have you been doing?' But I quite like being put in a position where I'm just free to do stuff. I quite like being accountable as well ... and when I'm occasionally asked to do a presentation about what I've been doing ... The feedback was useful to me because otherwise ... you're just this sort of wild-card roaming around, and I have a loyalty to the institution .... (late career faculty)

Thus just-in-time management, as the need arises, appeared to be the optimal approach:

> I'm lucky that my current head of department is very, very accepting of what I do – because I think it's been useful for the department and the university that they let me get on with stuff, so he's there when I need help. My dean of school is very, very happy with what I do and seems to let me get on with stuff, so it's very light touch in that sense but I do know who to speak to when I have a specific thing around either learning and teaching or research or policy stuff. (mid-career faculty)

A school academic manager

The following example of a head of school gives an indication of ways in which the process of facilitation at middle management level can work in positive ways, by generating and building on goodwill. At their institution a new vice-chancellor had devolved responsibility for making decisions in relation to local issues, and as a result, this head of school had been able to appoint their own management team which they saw as a positive development:

> I think when you have appointed people you've got different rules of engagement and relationships with them.

The academic faculty for whom this individual was responsible worked in practice settings, and much of their teaching took place in these throughout the year, as opposed to solely during term time. Many of the staff were part-time, and flexibility was required to meet the various constraints upon the school, including an institutional workload model devised for standard terms:

> We have given lip service to that ... [But] it has actually hindered flexibility and the management of staff ... I think it's about managing people on an individual basis.

Therefore the model had tended to be restrictive in relation to the types of development that might be made available to faculty:

> One of the challenges for me is how I give people new challenges, new responsibilities, that help them grow and develop, without getting stale, when within the workload system it's very sort of dominated by what grade you are and what the job is ...

More specifically, they had been able to modulate a performance framework that had been introduced at institutional level:

> Although it's been painful [implementing a performance framework related to the workload model] we have always had those things that we've ... called the annual conversation ... a conversation style dialogue that I've found much more helpful, because it becomes less threatening ... And then you move away from the hours and say ... how do you want to achieve this? ... So, putting the power into the course leaders to make the decisions about how they deliver ...

Part of the skill of this manager was being able to take the part of members of faculty, and understand their mindsets and motivations:

> there's the people that see work and home and everything integrated as part of their life and work is just part of life, and it's an equal part and an equal

responsibility ... Versus those who think, right, my contract says 37 hours, so that is 37 hours, and when that 37 hours is up, that's work forgotten about and put in its box ... I think it actually helps if you understand what kind of context each person works in, to try and enable them to feel satisfied in their work role, but also to keep them motivated ...

An example of this was a flexible approach to those with responsibilities for childcare:

I've got staff who are on a 0.8 contract but that ... enables them to work full time in term time and have some space during the holidays ... young children aren't young children forever, and sometimes this is a good compromise to enable people to fulfil their parental role, plus feel satisfied in the job, and not to feel they want to sacrifice one for the other.

Conversely:

in areas where they have been very rigid with their [workload model], then the goodwill and flexibility of staff is not necessarily there ...

Nevertheless, this manager admitted that being flexible could lead to issues of equity with other staff, which they tried to ameliorate by creating a 'trusting environment' across academic teams, and sharing out, for instance, unpopular working hours. Thus:

It's about trying to have some equality, but it's not necessarily about everybody has the same equal experience ... what I try and do is recognise what people don't want to do, try and mitigate it as much as possible, but when it has to happen ... look at the greatest good of the greatest number and think about how we do this in the fairest sense.

This person also gave priority to building a team environment, and drew on a sense of collective and shared responsibility, for instance in counselling individuals who for whatever reason were deemed not to be fully contributing:

once you have a conversation with somebody and talk about ... are you aware that people perceive you in this way re x, y and z, on the whole ... they buck themselves up ...

They also had a holistic approach to and broader vision of motivation and morale, which they saw as feeding into high quality institutional outcomes:

unless you give the staff a good experience ... the students aren't going to get a good experience.

This represents a more nuanced approach to what a member of the senior management team referred to as 'trying to get the behaviours to fit in with the strategy'. However, as this individual demonstrated, this is likely in practice to be an iterative process, with willingness to modulate expectations on both sides.

Support for middle managers

It was clear that a significant number of middle managers were uncertain about what the role involved until they were actually in it, with several expressing lack of clarity about precisely what was required, and how time-consuming it was. Whether they had had formal training or not, it was a largely question of learning by doing and building on experience. As one manager commented:

> we are really HR managers as well ... because we are responsible for [programme leaders] ... one of my [programme leaders'] lecturers is on probation, and there seems to be a lack of understanding of [mutual] responsibilities .... (head of department)

This was particularly the case in institutions that drew heavily on teachers from industry, the creative arts and the professions, where there could be issues about drawing together the contributions of sessional or hourly paid staff. Another common theme was the fact that the role tended to involve responsibility with what they saw as minimal authority:

> I became a programme director for the first time. That's a really extraordinary role, it wasn't at all what I thought it was; it's bizarre. It's a role that gives you loads of responsibility but absolutely no authority to do anything; so it's a co-ordinating role and one that requires soliciting the co-operation of others (as opposed to instructing others) and that's a very interesting set of skills to develop and it's quite exhausting as well ... I [then] became deputy dean of the school. Now, that was another eye-opening change of responsibilities. Again, it wasn't what I expected it to be at all; it was all about dealing with people and problems predominantly. (late career faculty)

The following narrative from a head of school demonstrated how they had met a need for support by spreading the load of decision-making with colleagues:

> I wanted a proper, formal senior leadership team ... I needed to have a sounding board and it was to protect myself really. But I also felt it was very important to have a deputy head. I felt that it was important for me to have an ally, have someone in a senior position ... The senior leadership team meets every couple of weeks and I've tried, wherever possible, to lead things, but to give responsibility to people. (head of school)

There is a sense here of developing collective responsibility among local colleagues and peers. This was corroborated by another manager with a remit for teaching development:

> I'm responsible for managing a team of eighteen people at the moment and I've never had any management training, and I probably have very little aptitude for it, but I enjoy it and I think I learn from my mistakes and from my colleagues, who give me feedback, which is a similar approach I take to teaching ... I don't do any of this on my own, so that's another key issue, I have to collaborate with people and I enjoy collaborating with people. (late career faculty)

This reflects that fact that learning on the job in a supportive atmosphere appeared to be valued as much as, if not more than, formal training programmes. Therefore despite provision of leadership development, coaching and mentoring for middle managers, a more holistic approach, incorporating day-to-day needs, is likely to be an ongoing aspiration as new cohorts of local managers are appointed. This is corroborated in other studies:

> Individualised training programmes, rather than generic 'all must attend' courses, were perceived as far more useful and relevant (Floyd 2016: 176).

A desire for support was particularly evident in relation to contractual and performance issues, which could seem particularly daunting to people who were taking on people responsibilities early on in their career, for instance in the management of a teaching team:

> if I encounter somebody who isn't helpful, you know, even in a small teaching team, if you're in charge of it and they're not really pulling their weight or they're doing something wrong, I find it very difficult to criticise them or to get them to do it differently ... It's just not really knowing how to deal with that kind of situation because academia is strange in that we don't have to do it that often ... so when we do we are completely unprepared for it. (early career faculty)

Conversely, a lack of support even at the most basic level of, for instance, inducting new staff into ways of working, could create a lacunae that was not visible or measurable, but could have a disproportionate effect. One middle manager, with responsibility for subject leaders, noted a difference between levels of responsibility taken by these leaders for the welfare of new recruits. This might include, for instance, informing them about where facilities were, and monitoring the way they taught and assessed students:

> [a programme leader] amazes me that he is not aware that he is responsible for ensuring that his lecturer is, let's say able to assess ... when I first started teaching, you don't know who to turn to, but if your own line manager

> doesn't seem to think it's their responsibility to sit down with you ... it might say in the job description, you're line managed ... but what does that mean? (mid-career faculty)

This illustrates the discretion that there is likely to be around responsibilities held by local managers, even at the level of programme leader, despite the existence of training programmes, and that within this discretionary element there is scope for a vacuum to develop. Such a vacuum could lead to a deficit, not only in motivation and morale but also in performance and quality outcomes, all of which could be pre-empted via a duty of care by a line manager or mentor. While this vacuum is unlikely to be precisely defined or calculated, poor performance and outcomes will undoubtedly reflect badly on a school or department. This manager also went on to say that in practice effective local managers would be likely to make themselves aware of the needs and backgrounds of individuals and 'concentrate on the ones who seem to need ... more support', thereby interpreting the precise requirements of their job description to 'line manage' in a nuanced way, recognising areas that needed attention and making judgements about when to intervene.

There was however also evidence that senior management teams were beginning to recognise that managers with responsibilities for staff at school and departmental level could feel vulnerable, and that support for them was necessary:

> I do think investment ... in having the right sort of mechanisms, working with heads of department on their own confidence ... So ensuring that there are safe spaces where heads of department can simply just come out and angst about it ... Creating an environment where heads of department could come to you and say can I talk to you about this before I go off and do it, and will you be there on the other side .... (head of administration)

Furthermore, middle managers may become the senior managers of the future and carry forward an understanding of the significance of middle management roles. Supporting them is therefore likely to be an important component of institutional succession planning.

Conclusion

Local managers could be the turnkey for interpreting and actioning policy, as well as being the listening post for faculty concerns and aspirations, and a conduit for bottom up initiatives and suggestions. At its best this was likely to be a symbiotic relationship, and overall there was a sense of policy implementation having become a more relational process in which local managers had a critical role, with greater discretion:

> One of the things we're trying to do now is see what greater levels of autonomy we can give to [managers] so that they feel empowered to do their job. (vice-chancellor)

On the one hand, local managers were often able to achieve a more nuanced approach to implementation than the senior management team, and were proactive in interpreting policy rather than simply, as one middle manager put it, 'mediating between two polarities'. Feedback and dialogue were essential components of this. They could also be the catalyst for individual career development by, for instance, negotiating structures and policies, achieving outcomes tailored to individual needs or strengths, and accessing local discretionary funding. On the other hand, this depended on the extent to which institutional policy could be modulated, and individual managers could also feel challenged in achieving individual solutions whilst maintaining perceptions of equity. In turn, the perceptions of middle managers about their roles could be equivocal, and they may themselves require support, both via formal programmes and day-to-day.

Thus, what might be termed a 'post-heroic' model of leadership appears to be emerging for middle managers, involving:

> multiple actors who take up leadership roles both formally and informally and importantly share leadership by working collaboratively ... Leadership can be distributed away from the top of an organisation to many levels .... (Turnbull James 2011: 19)

Similarly, in a higher education context it has been suggested that:

> The middle leader's role in higher education must be reconceived as being fundamentally and unquestionably relational in its entirety ... the middle leader's power and authority is more akin to influence and persuasion and is formed within a relationship with others built upon trust, transparency and consistency. In higher education, the role of the middle leader contains little trace of positional or coercive power and, thus, their authority is formed within the nature of their relationships. (Branson, Franken and Penney 2016: 142)

A study in a South African institution corroborates this, pointing to the fact that 'strategies that are more emergent in nature through processes that have a grass-roots orientation' are more likely to be successful, with a key role for middle managers (Davis, van Rensburg and Venter 2016: 1491).

The middle manager's role therefore might be represented as providing a nodal point within institutional structures (Ball 2008). In this sense it is as much an interactive role, with rank-and-file faculty as well as with senior managers, as an agentic one. The studies suggest that middle managers are in a position not only to join things up, but also to understand the implications of a specific course of action for an individual, their peer group, and their wider networks. There is a delicate balance for line managers in giving positive encouragement to individuals who are deserving, whilst also maintaining a sense of fair play, making sure that opportunities are communicated to all who might be interested, and being aware of those who are less articulate about their needs. This might be seen as a therapeutic aspect of their role. In order to develop a best fit between institutional requirements and individual strengths, therefore, the role of middle managers is likely to involve some form of integrative leadership (Sun and Anderson 2012; Hogg, van Knippenberg and Rast 2012). Not only do they have a key role in interpreting the policies and conditions in which individuals find themselves, but also in influencing these conditions, as well as responsibility for the way that individuals experience them. This represents an ongoing tension as individual managers are likely to have their own time and workload pressures, and may need support. They also operate within a broader set of relationships experienced by rank-and-file faculty, including teams and networks, which will be explored in the following chapter.

Part III

Towards a constructive alignment

Chapter 6

Emergent practices
Bottom up

The following three chapters consider ways in which bottom up and top down initiatives might be aligned so as to create a stronger iteration between structures and relationships. The idea of 'constructive alignment' was coined by Biggs (1996) to refer to the creation of an environment that supports learning activities in ways that lead to desired outcomes, and is therefore borrowed for this purpose. Since relationships are constantly shifting, however, alignment is likely to be an ideal rather than a fixed target, but there was evidence in the studies of individuals making things work in ways that at the very least achieved congruence of structures and relationships for specific purposes.

The studies aimed to bring into view practices and relationships that are informal and implicit as well as those that are formal and explicit. This offered an opportunity to review phenomena that may be perceived, at least initially, as peripheral to formal arrangements and, in research terms, as outliers in the data. However such arrangements may be instructive in shedding light on current developments, and also in pointing to possible future trends. This chapter therefore looks at practices and ways of working that might be described as emerging primarily bottom up from rank-and-file faculty, though they may also be mediated by middle managers.

Teams, mentors and networks

The influence of teams, mentors and networks was a prominent feature of the narratives in both studies. They might be described as the soft underbelly of institutional life, supporting and facilitating formal, collective workings, especially in contemporary institutions where working life is likely to be more dispersed, and people are less likely to cross physically in the corridor:

> you can feel as though you're not actually seeing people enough to have those sort of one-to-one conversations or little group conversations, which I think are more valuable than email conversations sometimes ... I feel

quite fortunate because I have got supportive colleagues, but often that's about me sort of going out and popping in to talk to them and it's a bit more informal ... I just feel quite strongly about having conversations and being mutually supportive within our departments. I think that's important. (mid-career faculty)

This also reflects conditions of 'new, more fluid working structures, networks, consortia and "hybrid communities"' (Henkel 2007: 197). In this context, social capital generated via informal and social relationships comes into play, and networks inside and outside the institution may influence and contribute to collective agendas, although they may not necessarily be acknowledged formally.

Teams

An investment in self-directed teams was a theme that recurred, and was exemplified by a manager on a professional contract, but with a doctorate, who had responsibility for employability initiatives. They split these responsibilities between three teams who, although co-located, were likely to be out and about working with employers and students. The teams each had strategic roles in developing the service, and were encouraged to engage in continuous dialogue about what they were doing. Every week this manager had a one-hour meeting with each team and a half-hour meeting with every member of staff so as to achieve continuity face-to-face. This led to 'a very transparent and quick transfer of information facilitated by cross team contacts'. They thereby aimed to create 'a stable environment with clear roles that provides opportunities for staff to progress within the service', and gave devolved responsibility to each of the teams. This represented a forward-looking strategy in that the team became empowered to maintain operations, for instance, if the manager took on other responsibilities. It also meant that the activity was not overly dependent on one person, provided development opportunities, and fostered lateral, peer relationships to provide future continuity. This person acknowledged that they themselves had a facilitative line manager who gave them the authority to make decisions and the freedom to experiment, and that this had helped them to develop a cohesive working environment. They therefore saw themselves as developing a client-oriented culture, with close relationships between academic and professional colleagues, which helped to mitigate inter-personal stresses and strains.

In an academic context, team teaching provided an opportunity to learn from peers in different disciplinary settings:

There is quite a lot of team teaching within the department, especially at the lower levels, so the first year modules are very large and they get team-taught ... you get to put on these team taught modules and you watch everybody else, so you can learn quite quickly. (mid-career faculty)

It also offered opportunities for constructive, one-to-one feedback via peer observation of teaching and action learning sets. As this was usually undertaken by academic colleagues, however, it could represent another time pressure on individuals.

In practitioner subjects, for instance as described by the following respondent in the health field, wider links with external teams were also seen as critical to the development of the discipline and practitioners for the future, as well as for sourcing funding and other opportunities:

> I had a team, a very diverse team, a team that was outside this university but the hub of it was here. The spokes went in all directions but it served me extremely well in my development. And I had a team who believed in me and invested in me and then that became more reciprocal as I grew and became interested in feeding back to them and working more with them ... understanding the bigger context, understanding how politics influence research, how strategy works is extremely important; the global aspect of research and not just your own ... world and your own discipline and your own subject area. (mid-career faculty)

This demonstrates the importance of a two-way exchange process that both reaches out and draws in people and knowledge, and thereby grows an area of research, and by implication a discipline, via a cross-fertilisation of ideas and practice. Conversely, the lack of a team environment could be a disadvantage, and as one person on a short-term contract noted, it was difficult for roles such as theirs to be integrated sufficiently to develop interdisciplinary synergy:

> there isn't really a sense of time and space for us to ... develop ourselves as a team of language and cultural studies teachers ... something we definitely don't have is any points of contact outside of our discipline, so a forum for that would be good. (early career, teaching-only faculty)

Mechanisms such as LEAN, a management philosophy about increasing value to the customer in products and services, were also used by some managers to break up structural silos and develop multi-skilled teams in which individuals could deputise for each other and also pursue their own portfolios. One respondent described how this had created collaborations by enabling people who had previously been restricted by structures to talk to each other. It had also reduced delays in decision-making by identifying what information was required and the people that needed to be involved, rather than necessarily going through a series of committees.

Mentors

A significant proportion of respondents in their early or mid-careers stressed the value of having a mentor, often informally, who not only supported and advised, but pushed them out of their comfort zone and enabled them to move forward into new areas of activity:

> one person I've remained quite close with is my PhD supervisor. We had a good working relationship throughout the PhD and if I want advice on teaching or ideas on teaching resources, because we work in similar areas, she's always happy to share her ideas or chat to me about what we should do and be very supportive.... (early career faculty)

Nevertheless, although helping early career staff with their future employability by providing opportunities has become an increasingly significant element of the role, senior staff may have difficulty in finding the time to mentor and advise their more junior colleagues, even on an informal basis (Austin 2010: 30). There was also recognition in the studies that ongoing guidance was likely to be required by mentors themselves, so finding individuals who had the time and motivation to act in this capacity could be a problem:

> one of the things that comes back time and time again when we have staff away days here [is] how ... do they support staff making wise decisions at different points in their career ... maybe there is, for very good reasons, there's good support for early career, but I think mid-career mentoring is possibly equally important, but who would do it? Who would take the time out of their schedules to do it? So those sorts of questions become really important.... (mid-career faculty)

There was also some evidence that formally appointed mentors could in practice be of less help than informal ones who offered just-in-time advice. This corroborates findings elsewhere that career discussions are all too frequently added on to the end of an annual review process with a single line manager, who may or may not be able to take appropriate action.

Networks

The studies demonstrated that broader networks increasingly supplement day-to-day team relationships, particularly in providing personal support and the exchange of experience. These often began at doctoral level, but also among contemporaries across institutions:

> there were a lot of people in the same situation as me, as young lecturers, first post ... so we all went through, regardless of our subject areas, similar sorts of experiences and being able to talk to young colleagues in what was ... a small institution therefore ... departmental barriers were quite a lot lower, and so as a cohort of young teachers I think we supported each other through the teaching quite a lot. (mid-career faculty)

Conversely, another respondent felt the lack of such a network, which could depend partly on discipline, partly on supervisor and partly on mobility:

> there are a lot of younger academics … who have maybe have done their PhDs at that university and their supervisor is still looking out for them, and they were doing research in areas that other people were doing research in, so there is that kind of mutually supportive network where they became aware of conferences, they're writing joint papers, they're doing joint conference presentations, they are meeting people, they're being introduced, their names are getting known in that really easy way. My research topic is quite obscure and there's nobody else, absolutely nobody here who does the same thing as me or anything that's even closely related to it. (early career academic)

This also points to the vital role of the supervisor in generating and stimulating the development of academic networks, and the incorporation of early career faculty into these.

Often it was simply a question of knowing who to speak to or who to go to for advice, which in large institutions was not always obvious, and many people valued their networks for this. On a day-to-day basis, time pressures often meant that peers were increasingly important in providing informal feedback on a just-in-time basis:

> the degree of peer learning that now has become just common practice … maybe ten years ago, the only conversation you would have had would have been to say, 'Would you read my article before I send it off and give me feedback?' Now colleagues are as likely to say, 'Will you read my portfolio for the Higher Education Academy, before I send it off, and give me feedback?' (late career faculty)

Internal development programmes could also lead to the emergence of local groups and networks, particularly among early career faculty:

> there's a nice network of people … from going on … these courses. (mid-career faculty)

In fact formal development initiatives, in-house or external, were often seen as most useful as an opportunity for extending networks and finding out what happened elsewhere, thus, 'about getting together and discussing and trying new things' (mid-career faculty). Others found it valuable to gain experience and contacts by, for instance, sitting on internal assessment panels for Higher Education Academy Teaching Fellowships.

Networks also fulfilled an important function in making contacts and developing ideas across disciplinary boundaries, which again could be difficult in contemporary institutions which might be dispersed geographically. This could be a powerful bottom up process:

> because I'm an ethnographer, they [the science department] found out ... and they started approaching me, so that was quite good for me because it gave me something to focus on, something to feel excited about, so what makes my day and motivates me to come to work and be satisfied is this new community that has formed around me in terms of both research and teaching topics as well – but that increases day by day ... it evolves. (early career researcher)

This sense of intellectual growth was one that recurred, with networks seen as providing synergy and stimulating ideas, as well as offering partnerships for research and other funding.

Conversely, a reluctance to be more interactive was mentioned by more than one respondent as being a problem for them, and that networking was a skill that they needed to acquire:

> my biggest problem, particularly in terms of how I research, is my personality ... It's a lack of confidence, it's my inability to self-promote and it's a difficulty I have in kind of networking, you know, of those kinds of things ... For me I think I went into academia because I just wanted to hide myself away in a book, and then you discover you can't actually do that any more, you have to self-promote, and I hate doing that. (early career faculty)

Nevertheless, this individual had, on the recommendation of a senior colleague, put themselves forward for a university committee and was using that as a way of developing interpersonal and management skills:

> I kind of felt like it was, well I said I would partly because I was, 'Well, he's asked me, I'd better', but then also I thought, 'Well this is my chance. I wanted to do this so let's be brave and do it' ... So that's partly why I've done it, to force me to actually speak up and develop in that way. (early career faculty)

External networks

There was widespread evidence in the studies of the use of external networks by individuals for their own support and development, from confidence building to creating productive opportunities. The Aurora women-only leadership development programme run by the Leadership Foundation for Higher Education (LFHE) was frequently mentioned by women as helping them not only to develop their personal portfolio, but also to develop social capital and role models:

> [the programme presenters] also include these little stories about career paths of women in leadership roles ... They went through how they started, and that's really valuable to see how they did it and you can relate and see that they aren't that different from me ... And I think that's really important, that was important for me to recognise that I'm not restricted to the people who are physically around me, but I can have my nurturing or temporal other groups. (early career faculty)

Aurora also appeared to be helping to counteract the fact that women tended to apply for promotion later in their careers.

At a more instrumental level, networks could also provide a source of information and indeed of future funding. Thus, one early career faculty had made a point of developing European networks to gain intelligence about topics of potential interest to funders:

> I'm a member of this trade body, so I go to quarterly meetings and that's a network ... across Europe, so that for me is really important in terms of networking, in terms of finding out what EU funding's going to be available, in terms of finding project partners and finding out what the new trends are in our domain. (early career, research-only faculty)

Opportunities such as secondments, exchanges and international experience were also seen as an opportunity to extend networks in a significant way.

The emergence of social media as a tool for communication has changed the landscape and broadened the scope of potential relationships in which it is possible for academic faculty to engage. For some it also provides an invaluable support mechanism that may not be immediately available in their institutions:

> I find Twitter amazingly supportive ... I didn't really expect it to be and it took me a while to get into it, but actually, just finding there are other people who have the same concerns or issues, or who are just generous and willing to share their thoughts about research practice.... (mid-career faculty)
>
> I probably wouldn't have stuck it [academic life] ... on Twitter there are so many other people ... Twitter gets together these lone people at different institutions to get a bit of critical mass, and so you find these online communities where other people write about similar things, and you think, 'Well I'm not the only one', and it's actually a bigger problem. (early career faculty)

Online networks may also help to overcome possible tensions arising from competition between individuals, for instance for advancement within the same institution.

There was also evidence that external networks were of benefit to institutions and provided a stimulus for innovation:

> I guess external relationships have been really helpful ... since that time [undertaking a PhD] I've been developing networks across the UK that have similar practitioners and researchers who are working in the area ... we chair a special interest group around ... [PhD topic] and learning. (mid-career academic developer)

Another respondent used links with business and industry to extend learning fora in ways that would inform students' future careers:

> my subject areas are business related ... mostly consultancy/research type activities ... I think we have a responsibility to be creative in terms of how people have access to that learning and that's not just about face-to-face delivery, online delivery, or whatever it is, but it's about different learning styles, it's about different learning environments, it's about workplace learning, it's about apprenticeships, it's about combinations of all the different learning approaches that our industry, our academic community, think about, create and develop. (late career faculty)

This makes clear the relationship between different learning locales and styles across the boundary of the institution and business partners. This person's role involved balancing these interests, negotiating and aligning agendas, and adding value to what the university could offer to students, regional stakeholders, professional bodies and specific industries. They called this process 'relationship recognition', which implies building a profile for activities which may have existed piecemeal, but had not been present in the collective institutional consciousness or policy making. It also involved meeting commercial clients' requirements, and overcoming procedural difficulties within the institution such as delays in signing contracts:

> where our commercial interfaces exist we have people, I believe, who are not ... sufficiently qualified also to engage with clients in the way that we are, solving their problems, not just undertaking research ourselves. (late career faculty)

The use of networks was generally seen as a benign influence, reflecting ideas about the involvement of broader constituencies in institutional decision making, so that concerns and risks can be addressed during policy implementation rather than *post hoc*, with a key role for middle managers not only as conveyors of policy, but also as enablers in generating commitment (Benington 2011; Ferlie, Musselin and Adresani, 2008). Furthermore, institutions that appeared to be relatively harmonious and at ease with what they were doing tended to have good lateral connections:

> I've always felt that the university has been good to me as far as support and everything goes and not just people within my department ... I've got to know lots of people around the university and some of it has been because of this outreach stuff. I've ended up working with people in the outreach departments and whenever I'm running events they are incredibly supportive. (mid-career faculty)

Such connections were on the whole facilitated by a cohesive structure, smaller rather than larger, and not too much of a geographical spread across sites. It has also been noted that networks and mentoring may be particularly valuable for part-time staff who may not be able to attend all meetings, and rely on networking with colleagues to keep up-to-date (Anderson 2007; Baxter 2010). Thus 'if inclusion and integration into educational values is perceived as important, then a more "relational relationship" – one that goes beyond contractual obligations – is vital', for part-time staff particularly (Bryson 2004: 32).

Networking and social capital – a delicate balance

Networking was seen by many as a priority for the purposes of self-development, and also to overcome isolation and achieve career advancement. This included having an online presence, blogs and publications, as well as attendance at conferences and working with more experienced colleagues in order to develop writing and presentation skills. As one respondent suggested: '... as soon as you get to certain higher levels, it's all about people and relationships' (early-career academic). This reinforces the view that 'the capacity to form supportive relationships at work is one of the main features of productive work environments' (Clarke 2015: 11). In some cases the social network (which might be said to represent an extended community of practice) was seen as more important to professional identity than other colleagues in the department. For instance, one person said that it had been a key factor in bringing in funding:

> The programme that I developed two years ago ... It's a part-time programme and that's brought in multi million pounds ... but it's only because of relationships I built up outside, not necessarily work relationships. (mid-career academic)

Networking can therefore be seen as a process that involves both building up and drawing down social capital in the form of disciplinary knowledge, professional contacts and thereby influence. It would appear to be critical, for instance, in the following description of early career academics at four universities in Sweden, who were distinguished by being 'invited' (recruited for research), 'useful' (recruited for teaching), both with associated social contacts and networks, and 'uninvited'. Thus, the latter had 'missed out on getting contacts and receiving help in finding the right career paths' (Angervall and Gustafsson 2015: 10) as a result of diminished social capital.

It was also apparent from the studies that extended networks could lead directly to assistance with career progression:

> I've had a lot of people help me through my career anyway, just gave me chances and stuff like that, so that's been helpful ... they actually backed me and hired me ... And supported me in what I try to do. So I have actually had a few people in the department gunning for me and supporting me in my research and giving me little bits of money here and there ... especially when you're breaking out, when you're a newbie, you kind of need that support. (mid-career faculty)

However, this person also hints at what might be seen as a less positive side of networks if they lead to perceptions of inequity and 'cronyism', for instance in the award of school or departmental funds for a project, or even additional increments or promotion. In terms of social capital theory (Bourdieu 1988, 1993) this could be seen as reinforcing and reproducing the success of those who have been successful in the past, with the potential for perpetuating selected groups:

> you get more cynical as you get older ... sometimes, if you've got the right person on your side, you can get pretty much any award. I've seen it in action, it does work; if you're friends with the head of department, they tend to push their group through and I've seen that happen quite a few times.... (mid-career faculty)

Furthermore, being proactive in building social capital could also create fracture points with colleagues whereby an individual might be seen as overly driven in pursuing their own agendas, as opposed to being a team player. Such a competitive element was demonstrated by one individual who said that they had been accused of:

> 'empire building' (like trying to collect ... accolades and things) ... [but] I need to do it to differentiate myself and my own academic career ... if there was more of a mentality of helping people collectively, that would be fine, I'd involve myself in that, but there aren't the mechanisms to do it, so you are left to your own devices.... (early career, research-only faculty)

This person also said that 'you have to know what to ask in order to get the correct kind of information [about career progression]', implying that being in the know was likely to involve personal contacts and information that might not be openly available.

Thus the narratives also suggest an ongoing shift towards a more competitive environment, between individuals as well as institutions, particularly among younger generations, as witnessed by one respondent:

> I'm fairly sure that getting a permanent job before I had my doctorate has meant that I've not had to be as sharp-elbowed as most people necessarily are, and that's made me less demonstrative ... I think you'd get a different profile and different type of behaviour out of many of my younger colleagues who just need to scrabble about with little posts, and they need to kind of crawl across each other to get ahead. (mid-career faculty)

This echoes Blackmore's view about the impact of competition between institutions on the potential for collaboration (Blackmore 2016), providing a counterbalance to, and indeed challenging, ideas about collaboration across teams and networks, and creating a tension of which middle managers in particular may need to take cognisance.

From networks to the portfolio academic

The following case example illustrates an increasing fluidity of relationships, and the significance of these for individuals and institutions. This individual worked on part-time and hourly paid contracts between different universities and industrial partners on knowledge exchange projects, as well as running their own business. In practice they had constructed a framework of relationships, which they inhabited and saw as their own, unique, space. They might therefore be described as 'portfolio' faculty, moving in and out of roles associated with different institutions.

I originally qualified as a civil engineer ... and I worked in the industry as a contractor for three years and ... I then decided to ... go back into academia and did my PhD ... and from there I stayed in R&D but in the commercial world ... I just wanted a change really, a bit of a career move ... we already had links with [x university] ... in fact one of my jobs there was to be the liaison with the university, because we had a number of joint projects, so it was a fairly simple move to enquire whether there were any possible vacancies at the university.

They weren't advertising for anybody but they had some projects on and some spare money for them, so they took me on on a fixed-term contract at the time ... I'm quite lucky in that the person that I knew at the university who was my contact when I came in, is ... somebody quite senior, and he is my line manager. So I've pretty much got free rein to do what I need to do as long as the money's there ... So it's not research for the sake of generating lots of knowledge and writing lots of papers, it's helping companies with development, and ... there are spin-offs from that where we can write a paper or two into the broader research programme we do, there's a lot of it that will be answering technical questions and advising our clients ... my role in that was helping to set up the tests and then I'll be analysing the results and writing the report. So there is interesting work that comes out of it, potentially some research, but ... a lot of it is commercial consultancy type work.

I then do a little bit of lecturing at [university of y] ... And ... I'm involved in the research down there ... because when I left my last job, [a few] of us set up our own business as an R&D consultancy in the [engineering] centre ... so when I go down to the university sometimes it's wearing a university hat and sometimes it's wearing my own company's hat and we work a lot with the students ... and I come in basically as [the university's] industrial adviser ...

We had three different workshop meetings [at the university] to discuss how they were going to increase their research output in future ... it was quite clear that there was a huge gulf between what was wanted from the top and what the people around the table were reporting back, which in my case was, 'Well with all the commercial consultancy there's not a lot of time for other research'. Everybody else was saying they were involved in teaching and that '[b]ecause of teaching there's no time' ... I am involved in the commercial consultancy work where you've got a client saying, 'We did our testing three weeks ago. Where's the report?', so you have that versus, 'I've got a pot of money to spend by next July, on some long term research', so you know, which one comes first? ...

I think the whole bureaucracy of the university is something that ... generally holds people back there ... Because I only do two days a week I feel it's quite a relief when I'm not there, when I'm actually working for myself, when I'm my own boss for two and a half days a week, effectively, minus a bit of time at [university of y]. It's quite nice to be able to say, 'Well I can make the decision to do this', and the research programme that we've got going within my own business, which has some activity at [university of y], we're doing a bit of work at [university of z] as well, so we're spread out in a few different places. I feel it's great having the freedom to make the decisions and to be able to do what I want ... If I want to spend money in my own business I get the chequebook out and that's it. If we need more money, I find more clients and send the invoices out ... You have far greater control and you don't feel you've got several tiers of management up above you who aren't really, I don't think, facilitating anything, they're just doing their jobs, day by day, meeting each week, meeting each month and so on ... So I'm almost a self-contained little unit of my network of my clients that I've brought with me and I'm working there within the university, and if I want to grow that and do something with it, now I can, and I don't think anybody is going to stop me.

At a descriptive level, this case study illustrates some of the key contextual factors for contemporary universities including a focus on knowledge exchange, commercial partnership and regional collaboration, as well as tensions that can arise between research and consultancy, ways in which research can become squeezed by teaching loads, and frustrations with rigid processes and structures, seen as causing delays and loss of business. At a conceptual level it illustrates the use of social capital combined with both serendipity and proactivity in obtaining a post in academia, together with the multiple belongings that this individual has within and outside the university in which they have their main part-time contract, the overlapping nature of their networks, and the porosity of individual boundaries. They ally themselves with academic and industrial colleagues in their team, and their relationship with the universities that employ them becomes something of a formality as long as they bring in research and consultancy income. For this individual, this is seen as an advantage, although they go on to note that it can be a disadvantage for others who are more dependent on structures. For instance, there may be a disconnect between formal annual review processes and specific career development opportunities (although this may be despite the good intentions and indeed the beliefs of institutional managers):

> I'm quite surprised ... that individual staff don't have their own development plans and training plans that they discuss with their line managers, but there's nothing like that [in the university]. In my previous job [in industry] I was expected to be able to talk about where I saw myself in five years and what the opportunities were and what the barriers were going to be and what training I needed ... [The university] have reviews each year but I don't think anything is taken from that in that they don't have their own career development plan ... I think if you were relying on the university to advance your career, to provide you with a rope to pull you up the wall, it's not going to happen. (research-only, portfolio faculty)

The case example also illustrates that, for some individuals, a market-oriented environment, in which the individual is thrown back on their own resources, may in some ways be seen as more nurturing and supportive than the relative 'safety' of an institutional environment. They may ultimately feel that they have more control over their careers, particularly if they have strong networks, are in an expanding field, and have built a solid portfolio of experience. In this type of career environment, it has been suggested that in the future, 'long-term professional progression' may need to focus on 'personal growth and social and intellectual contributions, rather than permanence and status' (McAlpine 2010: 2). This may in practice occur by default. This particular individual might be said to have the best of both worlds with the security of institutional employment for their teaching, and the opportunity to develop their own research and consultancy interests through personal networks in an industry in which they were well known and had a track record.

The relationship between the individual with their industrial colleagues, and between the higher education institution and the industrial partner, might be

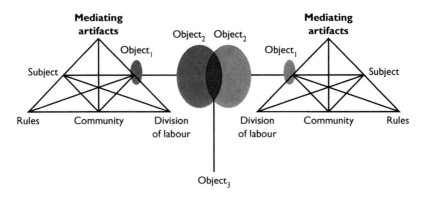

Figure 6.1 Engeström's 'third generation' activity system (Engeström 2001: 136)

theorised in terms of Engeström's 'third generation' activity system, with the two systems co-existing and interacting:

The concept of an activity system is based on the premise that the individual does not act in a vacuum, and is used to describe the relationship of individuals with the socio-technical systems with which they interact. It has been applied to the workplace to understand the influence of structural factors such as artefacts, policies and processes, as well as work communities such as networks, colleagues and teams. These interact to influence the outputs (objects) and outcomes, which may be perceived differently by different constituencies. Bringing together two activity systems, as in two collaborating organisations, therefore involves developing understandings about ways in which the contributory factors of both systems might interact to produce outcomes that neither could achieve alone.

Using Engeström's model, the components of the two activity systems, the university and the industrial concern, might be described as in Table 6.1.

The relationship between the five components of each activity system is dynamic, with multiple voices having different points of view, traditions and interests, and each system may be embedded within other systems, past and present. The objective, the testing of the industrial system, involves sense- and meaning-making by the actors concerned, which in turn are likely to involve elements of surprise, interpretation, ambiguity and potential for change. Part of this will be working through structural tensions within and between activity systems (Engeström 2001), including for instance those arising from a business environment interacting with a public service environment. Rather than seeing contradictions as problems and conflicts, Engeström sees structural tensions as sources of change and development, essential in progressing towards new practices and outcomes:

> multi-voicedness is multiplied in networks of interacting activity systems. It is a source of trouble and a source of innovation, demanding actions of translation and negotiation. (Engeström 2001: 136)

Table 6.1 Components of the university and industry partner activity systems

Activity system component	Case example: university	Case example: industry partner
Subject	Academic researcher and their ideas	Industry engineers and their ideas
Object[ive]/outcome	1 Consultancy 2 Innovation applied to industrial system 3 Research and development, knowledge exchange	1 Testing of industrial system 2 More efficient industrial system 3 Research and development, knowledge exchange
Mediating artefacts/tools and signs	Contract with industry, knowledge exchange strategy; critical path/project plan; documented precedents; written communication among team	Contract with university, strategy for bringing product to market, patenting; critical path/project plan; documented precedents; written communication among team
Rules	Legal and regulatory framework around technology transfer, patenting	Industry standards, legal and regulatory framework around consultancy
Community	University researcher team, academic department, line manager	Industry engineer team, line managers, customers
Division of labour	Research and development; innovative problem solving	Bringing product to market

Such translation and negotiation is likely to take place not only between institutional and industrial researchers, but also across their teams, and by team leaders and line managers responsible for those teams. These relationships are therefore critical in achieving 'transformation' and the emergence of 'object 3', which in the case example is the emergence of mutually beneficial research and development and knowledge exchange activity, in the joint interest of both the university and industrial partner. In the journey towards this outcome both are learning from the other:

> An expansive transformation is accomplished when the object and motive of the activity are reconceptualized to embrace a radically wider horizon of possibilities than in the previous mode of the activity. A full cycle of expansive transformation may be understood as a collective journey through the *zone of proximal development* of the activity ... [ie] 'the distance between the

present everyday actions of the individuals and the historically new form of the societal activity'. (Engeström 1987: 174; 2001: 137)

Although this is a specific example, it also illustrates broader changes to the dimensions of academic life. Of the 34 respondents in the Higher Education Academy study, who were selected to represent a range of rank-and-file faculty across types of institutions, career stages and discipline, sixteen, ie nearly 50%, had close external links on which their academic roles depended. For instance individuals played an active role with professional and disciplinary bodies (as opposed to simply having membership); business and industry; professional practice in the public and private sectors; the Royal Colleges; government, regional and community agencies; the NHS; charities; and international partners. Five of these individuals had other employers as well as a higher education institution, so effectively had portfolio careers. Among the other 50%, individuals had external links, for instance teaching in practice settings or undertaking outreach activity, as part of their day-to-day academic role. It can therefore be argued that institutions and individuals within them encounter new activity systems on an ongoing basis, albeit at different levels of formality, and that this is likely to involve what Engeström describes as 'collaborative envisioning' and 'expansive learning'. These activity systems are likely to be outwith formal structures and may not directly involve representatives of the senior management team.

In a microcosm this also illustrates the positioning of higher education institutions as serving the public good and being publicly accountable, and as businesses that are innovative and responsive to the market. In this case example, the situation works in practice because the industry line manager made the contact with the researcher and knows their history, and the team and their project have sufficient critical mass to persuade the university of the cost benefits. It illustrates the significance of both building and being able to draw on social networks and capital, and of being able to co-ordinate organisational systems, actors, networks and artefacts. According to Engeström, a key stage in bringing activity systems together is likely to be in the anchoring and co-configuration of the systems:

> Perhaps the most crucial form of anchoring in co-configuration work and expansive design happens sideways. This implies that the emerging new instruments are negotiated and shared in use with partner activity systems, above all customers or users ... Joint story telling, or co-narrating, is a typical action used to achieve anchoring sideways ... To facilitate such sideways anchoring in design, specific 'trading zones' may be constructed (Galison 1997). These are physical and discursive spaces that offer neutral ground for exchange between members of different activity systems. (Engeström 2005a: 15)

In universities, these 'trading zones' are likely to include, for instance, space for activities associated with knowledge exchange, partnership with business, employers and the community, and international links. A key element in this anchoring and co-construction is likely to be communicative relationships. At the same time, a danger for these types of arrangements is that communication between them in the 'zone of proximal development' is under-developed and *ad hoc.*

Conclusion

This chapter illustrates practices that occur bottom up, regardless of formal structures and processes, including the use of teams, mentors and networks, and the emergence of portfolio working. Sometimes they occur by default, and tend to arise from individual perceptions of need and/or aspirations, representing ways in which individuals deal with the demands placed on them in contemporary environments. In some cases practice may be ahead of policy, and although there might be a time lag before policy catches up, practice can in this way have a bottom up influence. In that sense practice might be seen as a critical force for change, even if this is not directly articulated or acknowledged. Understanding these day-to-day realities is likely to help local managers in their interactions with faculty, in providing a link with institutional requirements, and in enhancing the psychological contract.

Chapter 7

Emergent practices
Top down

The Leadership Foundation (LFHE) study demonstrated significant efforts by institutions to accommodate a broader range of working practices and styles. Some of these were aimed at addressing policy issues and financial pressures, others responded to bottom up demand, for instance for more flexible working patterns. However, attempts by institutions to introduce employment frameworks that enable them to accommodate a range of individual requirements, as well as peaks and troughs in demand, have also been seen as creating a less secure environment (Times Higher 2012; University and College Union [UCU] 2010; 2013). An example of this is the use of annualised contracts whereby individuals are guaranteed a certain number of hours per year but not precisely when these may be required. A variant is the use of zero hours contracts, which do not guarantee numbers of hours, although no examples of these arose in the study. Nevertheless, both the LFHE and Higher Education Academy (HEA) studies also demonstrated genuine attempts to respond to individual circumstances, as well as the general well-being of the workforce. Institutions are recognising, for instance, that the employment package as a whole assumes greater value in an environment in which they are less able to offer financial rewards. To this end, there were examples of imaginative forms of reward and career development to meet the aspirations of a more diverse workforce. Institutions were therefore responding to changing contexts, not only by adapting structures, but also in day-to-day practices.

The employment package as a whole

Examples of top down initiatives that were aimed at establishing a more facilitative employment package, and could be tailored to individual needs, are threaded through the chapters of this monograph. Gathering these together, they included:

- Benefits associated with adjustments to contracts such as flexitime or term-time only working, off-campus working, and nine-day fortnights.
- Trade offs between pay and leave entitlement, salary sacrifice schemes, for instance to pay for child care, and planned career breaks.

- The use of titles such as associate professor or director of teaching and learning at school or departmental level to recognise local responsibilities, and revised job descriptions for promoted posts such as senior lecturer.
- One-off bonus payments, pump priming funding, for instance on return from a career break, and non-financial rewards such as employee recognition and wellbeing schemes.
- The development of a range of career routes so as to allow a focus on different activities at different stages of a career, with the possibility of crossover at appropriate points.
- A creative use of workload models to take account of individual preferences and skills, and the balance of activity at departmental as well as at individual levels.
- Secondments and attachments, for instance to professional bodies or partner agencies, and the use of development programmes such as the UK Equality Challenge Unit's Athena Swan programme.

There was also evidence of variations to promotion criteria. For instance, increased student numbers and expectations mean that management responsibilities, even at the level of a module or programme, are more onerous, and individual members of staff expect to be offered credit for them. There are issues for entrants who have transferred into higher education from other sectors and encounter new sets of criteria, for instance in practice subjects. Furthermore, there are signs that people in fields such as knowledge transfer are increasingly marketable, and that attention to appropriate reward structures is key to attracting and retaining them. Such a broadening of criteria for promotion might recognise and reward, for instance, achievement in teaching, scholarship and pedagogical or practitioner research; introducing and/or leading a strongly recruiting master's programme; and links with professional practice, the community or the business sector.

The studies also confirmed the power of 'soft' reward mechanisms in the form of tokens of appreciation, such as celebrations of success, nomination for an institutional award, or a local book launch:

> So how do we celebrate…. recognition is giving praise to people, it's appreciating performance, appreciating doing something extra, which I don't think happens an awful lot. (director of human resources)

Thus, one vice-chancellor saw the Higher Education Academy National Teaching Fellowships Scheme as a positive motivator, giving academics 'a platform which gives them a profile. It may not give them a new job or more money, but they get positive feedback from their peers, and people love that'. Where this worked well, an appreciative environment was created:

> line managers have the option of nominating their staff for a variety of different awards, ranging through formalised thanking all the way through

to increased increments ... The other thing locally is that people in the department are very good at thanking you for stuff. If you've done a good job or you've contributed to something or you've done something to get them out of something that they couldn't do, people are generally very grateful and you can tell when it's appreciated. (mid-career faculty)

Nevertheless, there was at the same time evidence from the point of view of faculty that the 'feel good factor' arising from such rewards only went so far:

I don't want to belittle these things and there are various awards and marks of recognition, but nothing really that's as meaningful as a pay rise. (early career, teaching-only faculty)

Perhaps more significantly than the mechanisms themselves, such bespoke arrangements were described as 'hav[ing] a constant mode of negotiation rather than taking one fixed pattern and replacing it with another fixed pattern' (head of administration). In turn, this gives discretion to line managers to negotiate on what a director of human resources termed a 'something for something basis', in order to meet local needs. Such examples also demonstrate that attention to process, ie a discursive approach to what the possibilities might be, is likely to be as influential as the precise opportunities that are offered. However, they also bring into question issues of consistency and equity, and how these might be managed, even where different disciplines might require different approaches. For instance, a key tension existed around the extent of rewards that might be given for individual endeavour that went beyond the boundaries of a job description, which would imply innovation and creativity, and equity based on the precise performance of a role for which there were strict criteria and rewards:

we do have an 'in principle' decision to make about where is the boundary between the kind of job in which you make your way and if you're really good you are promoted on merit. And then jobs in which, in a sense, merit is defined by your performance in a role in a grade and there may well be merit payments or merit awards or commendations for excellent service, but the job is the job ... It's a sort of balance of contribution and individual aspirations being met. (director of human resources)

Thus, too close prescription of criteria with the intention of achieving equity could not only be frustrating for innovative and creative individuals, but also lead to a loss of talent to the institution if such people felt that they were unable to develop or progress.

Whatever new practices or modifications to existing practices were being introduced, a number of respondents stressed the importance of avoiding language that implied deficit, for instance that a focus on teaching and learning was compensation for lack of success in research, or an indication that remedial work was needed. A trade union representative, in a discussion around annual review processes, concurred with this:

> Just the use of language, 'performance management' ... The majority of our members will baulk at that, [but] if you start talking to them about professional development, career development, you can virtually have the same conversation ... How can I do what I need to do better, in a way that benefits me and is actually more interesting, and I think benefits the academy ... We could actually get to the same place by use of different language and a slightly different perspective and approach.... (trade union representative)

This person went on to suggest that trade unions could be 'positive actors in managing the process of change', for instance in developing partnership working. Collectively maintaining such a dialogue was also seen as critical by senior managers in institutions:

> We have a very good and mature working relationship with the University and College Union ... Basically, if they're not happy about something they will come and tell us. If we're not happy about something we tell them. And then we have a ... grown-up conversation about it. (director of human resources)

Another senior manager, a head of administration, also spoke of 'partnership' with union colleagues, encouraging them to 'share in solutions'. The relationship with trade unions might therefore be seen as a collective psychological contract, with a measure of informal understandings as well as formal agreements, conducted in a round table environment. The same director of human resources referred to the 'wider engagement of staff' via:

> Blogs, newsletters, campus gatherings, surgeries with senior people ... Those kind of things that put the human face on the institution ... You have a proposition because people feel engaged with the aims and ethos of the institution.

However, they also recognised that sensitivity to local contexts was needed, in that 'each department has its own slightly different way of doing things, its own norms ...'

Shared services and outsourcing

In the UK there has been significant interest at national level in developing new models such as shared services and outsourcing to achieve efficiency savings, while ensuring consistency and quality of service to students and stakeholders. A number of institutions have been experimenting with such models. Shared services involves two or more institutions jointly offering a service or facility, employing their own staff, whereas outsourcing involves paying an external contractor to provide the service or facility. A report by UniversitiesUK (2011) outlined what it saw as the benefits of a selective use of both. However, where the report referred to the 'engagement' of staff, this tended to be in terms of improving performance and the value of institutional services, with an emphasis on structure and process rather than relationships. A further consultation paper, with examples of collaborative initiatives in the sector, suggested that best practice was likely to be based on 'strong academic purpose that is underpinned by a sound economic rationale', with a 'strategic narrative' and 'shared vision' between partners, so that the impact on staff could be identified, agreed and communicated at an early stage (HEFCE 2012: 5–7). Again, in practice, the way that proposals for change were presented could be paramount, and middle managers were likely to have a critical role to play in achieving a positive process of implementation.

Perhaps because it is a smaller and more cohesive higher education system, there has been a significant amount of experimentation with shared services and outsourcing in Scotland. The Scottish Funding Council (Scottish Funding Council [York Consulting] 2007a and b) found that most institution-based examples were in the categories of learning delivery and facilities management. There were fewer examples in the areas of human resources, finance, marketing and staff development. There were also examples of collaboration between, for instance, colleges and universities, local authorities and the private sector. A Universities Scotland report (Universities Scotland 2011) identified issues that need to be managed by universities and stakeholders when assessing the viability of new initiatives. Although these included 'employee impact', they again focused on 'system' issues such as affordability, ability to deliver, risk and sustainability.

The use of such structural mechanisms to effect change leads into consideration of what might be considered 'core' and 'non-core' activity, and how far such models might be extended to, for instance, human resources, finance or student services, as opposed to discrete operations such as such as catering and maintenance. There were also questions as to whether this might enhance or detract from the overall employment proposition, and variables that might affect this, for instance institutional profile and co-location with other institutions.

Shared services, consortia and partnerships

Most sharing arrangements to date have been in discrete areas such as purchasing and information technology. A number of respondents made the point that the sector has longstanding examples of shared services at a national level, for instance the Universities and Colleges Admissions Service (UCAS), the Joint Academic Network (JANET), the Joint Information Systems Committee (JISC), inter-library loans, and the Universities and Colleges Employers Association (UCEA). Another model is exemplified by Jobs.ac.uk, which is owned by one institution that sells its services to other institutions. There have also been unsuccessful projects such as a UK initiative to design common software for management information in the 1980s.

Shared services may be out-posted to a service centre, be hosted by a partner, or jointly owned. As one head of administration put it:

> Shared services is a continuum from an institution designing services that others can buy, all the way through to a more integrated delivery model with everyone having an equal stake around it. The further you get to the latter end of that, the more complicated it is, because that's more about you visibly reshaping your own institution and doing it in a way that compromises with others.... (head of administration)

Perhaps for this kind of reason, others felt that sharing services could only be successful between institutions that had similar profiles, quality standards and business models, bearing in mind that institutions may also be in competition with each other. Success from the user's point of view is likely to depend on the degree of integration between different elements of service, so that queries can be re-routed, complex problems can be handled in one place, and individuals can deputise for each other. Relationships, therefore, are likely to be of the essence. Local managers may need to deal with equity issues arising from the use of different terms and conditions for staff employed by different providers, boundary disputes around roles and responsibilities, and tensions over sharing or rotating staff. Furthermore, a focus on operations and outcomes in the interest of greater efficiency may prevent a more holistic view, involving staff aspirations, from being taken. On the other hand, the use of higher education consortia for specific purposes may also provide opportunities by offering experience in different settings and with different teams. Motivational and ownership issues have been addressed in some cases by the development of a partnership arrangement with existing employees, for instance as an alternative to redundancy. In one such case in the studies there was a sense of doing what was right for the institution, and had local credibility.

However, the potential savings of shared services between institutions could be outweighed by additional overheads, and practicalities meant that this model was more likely to be successful in large conurbations. Furthermore, sharing was often driven by the needs of students following joint programmes in different institutions for common provision of, for instance, web platforms and library and information services; or where students from different institutions are taught on the same campus. There were also examples of the joint use of IT infrastructure for student records, including registration and examinations, which raised questions of how the staffing structures might be standardised across institutions in order to facilitate cross-delivery of information:

> If you have three different sets of staff in three institutions, if they're delivering a standard service, then you're going to need them to be structured

and behave in a very similar way, otherwise that doesn't work.... (head of administration)

There was also a feeling that vested interests within institutions could militate against the use of shared services, especially if this was seen as signifying a loss of institutional independence in relation to financial or staffing issues.

Outsourcing

Outsourcing involves using an external contractor to deliver a defined service. Where examples in higher education exist, these tend to be in relation to, for instance, security, catering and facilities management. None of the institutions in the study had outsourced functions such as human resources, finance or student services, which were generally seen as integral to an institution's mission and operations. However examples were given of institutions that were planning to do so, particularly in large conurbations where there were likely to be other institutions to whom such services could be offered. Some institutions were looking at outsourcing of, for instance, IT services, student email and payroll, but according to one head of administration, 'nothing game changing'.

One respondent gave an example of outsourcing catering. Although the rationale had been to reduce costs, improve quality and efficiency, and attract capital investment, it had nevertheless had a positive impact on the student experience and the quality of service:

> we contracted with [a private company] ... they came to us with a proposal for future investment which would be shared ... So what they did was imagine the kind of service that the future student would want. [As a result] they needed to change the physical environment and the kind of food they served – more takeaway, more flexibly served ... So we improved the student experience by outsourcing. (vice-chancellor)

Although staff were required to transfer to the new provider, and were given new terms and conditions, all stayed with the institution. Other respondents felt that ensuring the quality of the student experience and consistency of provision and care (for instance in relation to campus services) militated against outsourcing to providers where there was less direct control in relation to providing a rapid response if problems occurred:

> We've got a large estate, critical mass. Whether we would ever move to [outsourcing] in the future is a pertinent point, because effectively we do know that we pay above market rates for certain key functions. But then in terms of the benefits of moving away from employing the people ourselves, it's more

than just a financial decision … it's the wider business case as to why you would want to do that…. (director of human resources)

Another example arises from a privately run centre for study skills and language programmes, with the university maintaining control over academic matters. This centre used annualised contracts but gave permanent status to staff who could choose the number of hours they wished to work each year. The manager of the centre described this as a partnership approach which included sharing profits. In this case language teachers had transferred from the university, some preferring to work part-time, as it enabled them to pick up different types of work, including private consultancy.

Although these types of arrangements may have been introduced in the first instance for the purposes of efficiency and the enhancement of services through resource sharing, they have had a significant impact on relationships, which were a critical element in their success. Using the concept of Engeström's activity system, as described in Chapter 6, as a frame (Engeström 2001), components might be as laid out in Table 7.1.

The interface between the institution and other providers is one that needs to be managed carefully to develop space in which dialogue can take place, relationships fostered and joint objectives and outcomes agreed. In cases where arrangements, particularly outsourcing, were less successful, a contributory factor was likely to be the robustness of this area of communication and the effectiveness of agreements around, for instance, quality standards, as well as the confidence that each party had in the other. Thus activities requiring an investment in relationships such as those of teachers with students, or human resources professionals with employees, which are less likely to be a high priority for commercial providers, may be considered less suitable for outsourcing. In this respect partnership arrangements might be said to represent a halfway house.

However, as shown by Blackmore (2016), competitive relationships between institutions can also militate against shared or consortia-based services, and are likely to be a consideration in decision-making. Thus at one institution the director of human resources explained how a new contract had been introduced via lengthy discussions with individuals which had not been 'pain-free', but the investment of time had been seen as an important element of the process so as to understand individuals' concerns and provide assurances. Partnering arrangements also created the need for link people at middle management level to ensure that joint working met required standards and criteria. This in turn can 'shift the internal dynamics' (Sloan 2011) and demand skillful handling on the part of local managers of issues which may be neglected at the level of institutional policy making, especially if, for instance, staff work for different institutions with different terms and conditions. In some cases the strain may be too great and result in arrangements being dissolved.

Table 7.1 Components of activity system relating to partnership and outsourcing arrangements

Activity system component	Institution	Examples: employee partnership/ institutional consortia	Examples: outsourced facilities and maintenance/ language teaching
Subject	Director of service e.g. facilities, language centre, library and information services	Director of e.g. employee partnership/ institutional consortium	Business manager
Object(ive)/ outcome	1 Enabling institution to focus on academic matters 2 Improved effectiveness in use of resources 3 Quality service for students and stakeholders	1 Improved staff morale/security of employment 2 Effective use of resources 3 Quality service for students and stakeholders	1 Successful business 2 Preferred provider status 3 Quality service for students and stakeholders
Mediating artefacts/ tools and signs	Legal contract with providers; quality targets; service level agreements	Service and user manuals; codes of practice; IT provision; facilities and equipment	Equipment and materials; service contract and performance indicators; on site facilities
Rules	Legal and regulatory documents	Heads of agreement; custom and practice	Heads of agreement; quality and maintenance targets
Community	Senior management team; professional services; faculty and students	Institutional governing body; governing board of service; faculty and students	End-service users; staff and students
Division of labour	Negotiation and monitoring of contracts and outcomes	Delivery of service; maintenance and monitoring of quality standards/ outcomes; collaboration with partner institution	Delivery of service; maintenance and monitoring of quality standards/ outcomes; liaison with institution

Private providers

As early as 2000, Coaldrake identified new educational providers in the United States who were:

> contracting separately with a group of academics to develop a curriculum, sometimes in consultation with industry clients, and then with another group of people to teach the curriculum ...

arguing that:

> experts at the cutting edge of new knowledge are not necessarily the best at teaching students, nor do they necessarily possess the requisite practical experience in vocationally-relevant disciplines. (Coaldrake 2000: 12–13)

Such institutions tended to be client-focused and to restrict their range of courses to those in fields such as business, information technology, law and engineering. Although such arrangements are not mainstream in the UK, the Government White Paper of 2011 included a new policy that students taking programmes offered by private providers that had been designated by the Secretary of State as eligible for student support might receive fee loans, maintenance loans and grants, in the same way as students at public higher education institutions. Private institutions may therefore feature more prominently in the future. They tend to be characterised by staff with a teaching-only brief, and staff turnover can be high. Furthermore:

> they often have extensive experience as academics in traditional universities (and some work in both sectors) and as practitioners in a variety of professional fields in different sectors and countries. (Middlehurst and Fielden 2011)

Some private providers may in the future have ambitions to allow their staff to undertake research, particularly vis-a-vis practice. Although offering a different product from traditional universities, it has been argued that private institutions are 'having an impact on traditional academic practices and affecting recruitment and retention patterns, academic standards ... and managerial culture' (Blass, Jasman and Shelley 2010). All these factors in turn create, or have the potential to create, new forms of employment relationship with the institution and working relationships between colleagues.

However, within the one private institution where interviews were undertaken, a lack of social capital across wider disciplinary networks was evident. For instance one respondent said that since being in the private sector they had not been asked to undertake external examining in the public sector. This may be because in the

UK the private sector is as yet small, but it indicates a cultural barrier that may emerge as the private sector expands, particularly as private institutions tend to focus on subjects that bring in a regular income stream, and with which they and their faculty are closely aligned in terms of purpose and identity. This more business-oriented approach contrasts with the many informal relationships on which public sector institutions in the UK depend. However, as shown in Chapter 3, public institutions in the UK may contain elements of private sector approaches, often in relation to specific programmes. This is a trend that could increase as more private institutions are established for specific purposes, especially if they are successful in attracting publicly-funded students.

Structural challenges to relationships

Some examples of shared services and outsourcing are mainly characterised by structural and process considerations, with less potential for an impact on relationships. Others have greater impact on specific groups or categories of employees. Generally, changes that introduce contractual distinctions have the potential for straining relationships, be they between different categories of staff working for the same employer, or, albeit less commonly, staff working on the same task but primarily contracted to a different employer, be it another university or private provider. Three examples of collaborative activity in various forms illustrate some of the challenges.

In the first, two institutions might form a new organisational unit to meet a specific need, for instance widening access. Both institutions will want to be actively involved in the teaching and will tend to seek willing volunteers. Over time, the partners may form a revised view of how the initiative sits with their overall strategy in terms of the policy focus on widening access. If one partner sees it as central to the whole ethos of the institution, it may emerge that the specific initiative strains rather than strengthens existing relationships.

A second illustration arises from the situation when two institutions take collaboration to a stage that involves combining course or subject provision. Administrative arrangements will ensure who is responsible for what, but that cannot guarantee that stresses and strains will not occur, even when both sets of academics supported, at least in large measure, the establishment of the initiative. An added layer of potential for difficulty can occur where members of the combined department remain contracted to their pre-combination employer. Thus, any dispute or complaint has to proceed through the channels of the contract issuer, even if the dispute involves staff employed by the other institution. It can be difficult for such arrangements to avoid frictional drag, detracting from the anticipated reputational and development benefits. Internal reorganisation is also likely to have a disturbance cost in relationship terms. Indeed part of the policy implementation challenge is to find a means of reducing loss of effectiveness and engagement from such structural disturbance.

The third example involves an institution which consists of several separate colleges, each of which retain their identities and employ their staff, in addition to contributing to the degree programmes and, progressively, the research of the university. Mutual respect is a core dimension of relationships and that is constantly put to the test, as indeed it is more generally in mergers and multi-institutional collaborations. Key variables include the fact that institutions differ in detail in terms of history, structure, development and aspirations. The basic building blocks may seem similar, for example academic departments and supporting administrative functions, but even these can conceal considerable variation. For example single subject institutions are still commonplace in some countries. They would appear to stand at the opposite end of the spectrum from large multi-discipline universities. Another category includes multi-campus universities, many of which came into being by the merger of distinct institutions. Overwhelmingly the 'new' institution that is the outcome of merger(s) becomes the employer of the staff and over time seeks to develop a coherent and cohesive set of policies. However that can take time to achieve, especially when significant contractual differences have to be resolved, let alone enabling time for prior cultures, customs and practices to settle in to change organisational relationships. For instance, when independent teacher training colleges became part of universities, both in the UK and elsewhere, they brought considerable strengths in relation to their expertise and practitioner development, and their strong networks with schools and practising teachers. The contracts of staff, at least in part, reflected these historic links, most visibly in terms of the work expectations placed upon staff outside term time. In philosophy that may not have been different from the understanding that university staff would be able to focus upon research and scholarship outside term time, but the contractual realities were significantly different, and often took some time to harmonise.

The list of potential organisational relationships continues to grow, embracing, for instance, the incorporation of international companies, branch campuses, international consortia, joint degrees, international research projects, massive open online courses (MOOCS), employer/institution links, community/institution links, professional body/institution links and software/publishing company/institution links, as well as the possibility of future mergers, resource sharing and outsourcing. In practice, some initiatives are likely to fail or falter, while others emerge and flourish.

Conclusion

On the one hand, institutions are becoming more pliable in their recognition of the advantages of creative approaches to the employment package as a whole, with a range of mechanisms available to local managers to flex formal contracts in ways that play to individual needs and strengths. On the other hand, they are also experimenting with structural changes along a continuum of collaborations, shared services and outsourcing, often arising from resource pressures, although such initiatives have tended to be adopted cautiously. Although discrete and relatively contained activities such as facilities and catering can in certain circumstances be run as a separate enterprise in this way, concerns were expressed by a number of senior managers about the impact that this could have on the relationship with staff and students.

Sharing academic initiatives across institutions is likely to have inherent stresses, for instance two sets of policies and procedures for groups of staff employed by different institutions, unless both can be closely harmonised. Large consortia add to this complexity. Friction that arises may be seen as too costly. Shared academic provision is more likely to be successful if this is seen to benefit students, is valued by staff, and perceived by managers to enhance the institutional profile. For instance, potential savings on functions such as human resources and finance were generally viewed as being outweighed by the advantages of a more personal service, with known staff members and the potential for face-to-face contact. As one senior manager commented, 'every touch counts' in building an institutional culture which makes the institution a rewarding place to work and feeds into relationships with students.

Thus, although attempts by senior management teams to achieve greater flexibility of structures top down may be aimed at accommodating the needs of a wider range of faculty, they can also result in arrangements that may be perceived as less secure, and as lacking clarity and transparency. Relationships may become less predictable and therefore less dependable, so that empathy and support is sought elsewhere, for instance with teams, mentors and networks. What was clear was that whatever the model, making it work was likely to depend on relationships constructed by local managers, involving the interpretation of policy but also listening to the concerns of individuals. Chapter 8 will demonstrate how effective policy development and the emergence of new practices is likely to be an iterative and dialogic process involving a broad mesh of relationships, which may at times involve the adjustment of structures and processes so that they catch up with practice.

Reconstructing relationships

It was apparent from the studies that the reconstruction of relationships was an iterative process, involving articulation of needs and aspirations by rank-and-file faculty and listening skills by both middle managers and senior management teams. Some changes were happening incrementally, almost by default, becoming incorporated locally as part of implicit agreements, and then being formally rationalised into policy *post hoc*, with policy moving forward on that basis. This process has been accelerated by a more diverse workforce than even a decade ago, including, for instance, those in professional practice subjects, professional staff working on academically-oriented agendas, and individuals on segmented contracts that might, formally at least, focus exclusively on teaching, research or knowledge exchange. This has also led to a broader range of contracts, rewards and incentives, career paths and professional development requirements. Many of these requirements are managed via annual review processes and informal conversations over time, along with opportunities for development. Acknowledgement and recognition of individual circumstances are a key element in building and sustaining positive relationships, which in turn enable policy renewal, even if the action it is possible to take at any point in time represents a step towards, rather than the precise achievement, of a goal. This chapter considers examples of good practice of building relationships via such an iterative approach.

Constructing facilitative relationships

The narratives in the two studies suggest that increased regulation within the sector, together with greater codification of institutional policy around working conditions, has generated a stronger requirement for their flexible interpretation at local level, and that this is likely to be underpinned by implicit understandings which oil the wheels of day-to-day activity. Thus:

> We don't prescribe a kind of flexi-working policy. We very much leave it to individual departments to work within their own guidelines ... we don't have a formal home working policy, deliberately so, because once you make it formal then you have to enter all kinds of constraining contractual features. (director of human resources)

The most effective examples of good practice demonstrate institutions being facilitative in relation to, for instance, progression and careers, rewards and incentives, workloads and performance review, without being overly prescriptive. At the heart of this is the creation of discretionary space that allows individuals to understand and realise their potential, for instance carving out their own niche within a local context. In some cases individuals may find in this discretionary space some of the freedom they may feel they have lost in a more performance-driven environment. In some institutions this appeared to be managed within formal structures in which the majority of staff were expected to undertake both teaching and research:

> [Teaching-only contracts haven't] happened yet but you can, without changing your contract, because of the three elements within it, you can negotiate what percentage of each element you do. So if you really wanted to focus on teaching, you could rack up your teaching hours and reduce your research hours, for example. If you really wanted to work in research, you could do the same, and if you wanted to work in enterprise you could do the same, as long as the needs of the school or the department were met ... So we don't need different contracts in that sense because there's flexibility there.... (late career faculty)

There were also examples of individuals finding such discretionary space themselves. For instance, in another institution, one member of academic faculty with a teaching-only contract suggested that this form of contract liberated them to undertake the type of research they wanted to undertake, in a way that they wished to do it:

> A lot of my research is theoretical, so my papers take a long time and ... when I do produce something I'm proud of what I've done ... I want it to be something that I feel I really am proud of and happy with, as opposed to I have to hit certain target journals and go with the pressures of the REF [Research Evaluation Framework] ... just because you have to jump through hoops, and I'm not particularly happy with that. So I love the fact of being able to produce what I can. (mid-career, teaching-only faculty)

Another institution, that appeared to have arrangements that were pliant in relation to individual working patterns and interests, had a vision whereby individuals could focus on different activities as different stages of their career, rather than trying undertake everything at the same time:

> I think where we're wanting to see things move in future is actually to start blurring some of those boundaries [between teaching and research] ... I think that there's more merit in ... having an [overarching] academic progression route, and you might be on the teaching end of the spectrum

at one point in your career, and you might move a little bit more over to one side or the other side of it, or you might duck out, or you might get recognised just for one part of it…. (director of human resources)

This would appear to represent a new way of thinking about a career in its totality rather than requiring a complete alignment of teaching and research at any one time, or prejudicing an individual's future by penalising an emphasis on a specific activity for a defined period.

Taking this longer view might require a strong measure of trust, but would appear to be motivating for individuals, and could be agreed as part of the annual review process. Although there is inevitably an iteration between generic criteria for promotion and progression and rewards for innovative or specific contributions, it would appear that there could be some malleability around this, and local managers would be likely to make such judgements and recommendations. The same manager went on to describe how local managers needed to understand this, and described the process as 'creative friction':

> we need to expect [some] bumpiness and be confident that that's okay, we're comfortable with that but we'll learn from it … we'll build the skill base, build the resilience, build the understanding from our managers and that, in time, should reflect better in the way we reward people. (director of human resources)

This reflects the delicate balance between mechanisms that reward for work done and those that motivate for the future, and the difference between the two. Ultimately, although discretionary awards may provide a short-term 'feel good' factor, career progression would appear to be more empowering to the individual. This may also reflect a difference between those who are primarily intrinsically motivated, those who are pragmatic, and/or those who are proactive and instrumental in pursuing their goals.

The link between relationships with mentors and line managers, an individual's professional and intellectual development, and annual review and reward mechanisms is shown clearly in the following:

> There is a mentoring scheme, there is appraisal, [and] we are all, as members of staff, attached to a kind of research adviser and … there's a kind of formal thing which is appraisal where this gets talked about, there's a formalised departmental thing about research, which is really seen as an intellectual thing, but obviously your intellectual development is keyed into your professional development, your promotion etc … It's all quite light touch but I don't think that makes it insubstantial. (mid-career faculty)

A concept that recurred among both senior and middle managers was that of managing expectations, for example in relation to the introduction of teaching and scholarship, as opposed to teaching and research, as a recognised career and progression route. One middle manager described this as a significant 'culture change' which could only become embedded over time as individuals went through the system, demonstrating that it worked in practice. Management of change issues also came into play, for example the creation of 'job families' as a technique to create a 'mixed economy' in relation to career paths. Another manager spoke of 'helping people understand their role and how they fit in', particularly in a team environment, thus making a positive investment in facilitating relationships, rather than necessarily expecting them to work by themselves. Team rewards were another mechanism for fostering peer relationships.

The two studies suggested, therefore, that the relationship between institution and individual involves a combination of the institution offering rewards, incentives and development programmes, and the agency of individuals in accessing them. This is an iterative relationship and where it works well there is recognition by individuals that there is an onus on them to take and even generate opportunities, using informal relationships and networks as well as formal organisational channels. The existence of dialogue, formal and informal, is likely to be a critical success factor, though that is not to say that access to opportunity should not be fair and transparent, and engender perceptions of equity. At the same time, in practice, some institutions and institutional segments attracted higher levels of earnings from, for instance, consultancy fees, research income and overheads, allowing more scope for individual rewards.

The listening institution – a case example

An iterative process in building constructive relationships was illustrated by an institution with what appeared from the narratives to be a well-supported group of staff who took advantage of what was available to them. There was a sense that the individual should be in the driving seat rather than the institution, allowing them to be proactive in seeking what they needed at any point in time:

> there is a big push if you like to recognise the individual's responsibilities for initiative and taking forward things, leading their own path, if you like, rather than tramlines. (academic developer)

The university had therefore integrated the development of management, leadership and professional skills for the spectrum of activities that might be expected of faculty associated with teaching and research at different levels:

> we're looking at transition between roles and the support that's needed for different roles and responsibilities, so we have in place a leadership and management suite [of programmes], which has mixed academic and professional services staff on it, to reflect the different roles that the groups are doing at any one point ... so there's interaction there. (academic developer)

From the university's point of view, achieving 'buy-in' for a development programme that could be internalised by individuals was seen as critical. Younger faculty were engaged by tying this into probation procedures. Thus:

> it's not saying, 'These are your options', it's saying, 'What do you need, what do you want? And can we deliver that?' ... we're looking at self-assessment diagnostics at the point of entry, so that we can then tailor development support for an individual ... even more ... like a 'playlist' if you like, of development that you might want to sequence over a period of time ... that's helped bridge that gap between what an institution needs and the way we can put it in place. (academic developer)

Being able to appreciate the practical aspects of what was intended as a comprehensive programme, and having confidence that this longer-term process would ultimately extend deep into the institution, was expected to have greater impact on individual expectations and institutional culture than one that was driven by, for instance, simply collecting attendance data:

> there is a wealth of support available once you start to access it and identify that you want it. But that motivation varies for different people and different times in careers when people may seek something out, and there isn't necessarily a pattern for that. (academic developer)

At the same time the institution was trying to reduce stressors that impacted on academic faculty, for instance, multiple requests for the same information for different purposes, such as staff review, teaching loads and research assessment:

> we're trying to tackle this on a number of fronts; on the psychological front we're trying to increase people's resilience, we're trying to help people manage workloads by improving processes and cutting bureaucracy ... We now have five or six or seven separate processes, forms, all of which are duplicating the same information ... So we're ... looking at ways of helping people to cut through that.... (director of human resources)

Less formal measures at local level, often involving a combination of mutual support and self-help, were particularly valued by individuals, especially if this was provided in response to a specific need and at an appropriate moment in time. It was clear that optimal value was more likely to be achieved if development programmes were closely tailored to individual needs, with provision of targeted support. Otherwise, as several respondents noted, it could become a bureaucratic requirement in order to demonstrate credibility and proceed to the next stage of a career. In practice, such matching was likely to require discussion and provision of appropriate opportunities supported by local managers, even though this may be initiated by the individual:

> what I'd like to put in for this term is to have maybe monthly drop-in sessions where myself and maybe the director of research, anyone can come

and just have a discussion of what's going well and what isn't and then we can maybe decide what training people need, based on those discussions, so have a more informal group. Because a lot of training tends to get thrown at new staff at the wrong times actually and it's not quite the training or the timing that's needed ... I think if we let them drive it that would be something really helpful. (head of school)

It was further suggested that development programmes that were designed to promote self-reflection could also instil confidence, which could often be an issue, particularly with women:

I do think ... getting staff to actually reflect ... at an early stage, then they take that through with them and they are more likely to engage with pedagogy and be interested ... I think it's good for their self-esteem as well, actually to reflect on what they've done. (head of school)

Individual departments were also encouraged to develop collective initiatives in relation to, for instance, attracting research funding:

[one] department have decided to go for a sort of model where they don't do lots of individual grant applications, they decided on a kind of thematic basis as a department what they will be doing. They get a range of colleagues involved in it and they've been very successful in developing that sort of model, and ... it's clearly very helpful for younger colleagues who might not have the standing or whatever yet, to get the necessary grants. (pro-vice-chancellor, education)

In turn, respondents valued opportunities made available to participate in cross-university activities and development initiatives in order to pick up information, learn from others and develop good practice. Others felt it had been important to establish a niche role, such as being the 'go to' person in their discipline for ethics advice or schools engagement.

Typology of relationships

Table 8.1 categorises the types of relationships and interactions arising from the narratives between rank-and-file faculty and their institution, their line managers and peer groups, and the activities that characterise these. *Obligatory relationships* are those that are required to maintain legal and regulatory aspects of the employment contract. These may be regarded as constraining, but they also protect the individual in relation to, for instance, terms and conditions of employment and considerations of equity. *Discretionary relationships* are those that are likely to involve local managers in interpreting and facilitating the formal employment contract in ways that play to local circumstances and incentivise individual faculty. An important aspect of this is communication, face-to-face, online and via social media. Support networks may also develop among peers, and can create bottom up pressure and influence. *Voluntary* relationships are those that are likely to be more personal and social in nature, based on mutual interests, both on and off campus, and may be seen as particularly useful for building social capital. Both *discretionary* and *voluntary* relationships allow, in differing degrees, autonomy and choice on the part of the individual.

Table 8.1 Faculty working relationships

Key players with whom individual faculty may interact	Obligatory relationships	Discretionary relationships	Voluntary relationships
Institution/ senior management team	e.g. Fulfilment of contracts Maintaining appropriate reward and recognition system Maintaining appropriate performance/ promotion criteria	e.g. All staff meetings Senior staff blogs/ social media Civic and regional engagement events	e.g. Social – annual all staff party Internal prize and fellowship events
Middle managers (e.g. deans, heads of school/ department, programme/ team leaders, line managers)	e.g. Work allocation to individuals and teams Annual review of faculty Departmental and programme meetings	e.g. Career counselling/ advice Provision of career development opportunities Manager blogs/social media Town and gown/ community events	e.g. Social – coffee, lunch, informal gatherings Sport/the arts, on and off campus Local memberships and civic events
Mentors/peers/ networks	e.g. Work-based team meetings Regular meetings with mentors	e.g. Sharing of information/ good practice/advice Membership of disciplinary/ professional body and/ or network Blogs/social media	e.g. Social – coffee, lunch Sport, the arts, wellbeing on and off campus Social media Local memberships and civic events

The categories are intended to represent a continuum rather than being tightly bounded, and the activities in them to offer examples. They are not mutually exclusive and individuals are likely to be involved in all three types of relationships, accommodating to and adjusting these on the day-to-day basis. In particular, some activities may move between the discretionary and voluntary categories according to the context in which they take place. The table is therefore intended as an illustration of what appears to be happening from the narratives, that there is an ongoing shift whereby activities undertaken as part of the involuntary and formal relationship between an institution and its staff are increasingly counterbalanced by those taking place towards the discretionary and voluntary end of the spectrum. Relationships are no longer entirely constrained by structures, and may be becoming less so. Rather than being based solely on a quantification of hours spent on specific activities, the relationship with faculty is increasingly likely to be reinforced by bespoke, often local, agreements.

How far formal relationships might be informed and influenced by local relationships is likely to depend on the receptiveness and responsiveness of the institution, its senior management team and local managers, as well as the interpretive and negotiating skills of individual managers. The success of negotiations may well depend on the conjunction of time and space and other contextual factors, including relationships that are forged informally. Within the discretionary and voluntary categories might be located the increasing reciprocity that exists in relation to, for instance, undertaking activities that do not 'count' in workload models, such as internal and external examining; chairing of committees, examination boards and vivas; internal reading of theses; and doctoral upgrades.

A 'favour' economy depends on mutuality and the building of social capital, for instance, if I do you a favour by acting as internal reader for your student's thesis, I can ask you at a later date to read my student's thesis. However, one of the results of a more marketised and regulated environment within institutions is that while such roles have traditionally been accepted as part of academic life, they may increasingly be subject to an individual cost–benefit analysis and calculation of reciprocity. Thus, it could also be argued that in current environments such favours may shift from being 'discretionary' (as part of a 'collegial' or common culture) to being 'voluntary' (as part of a calculation of something for something). A 'favour' economy may also be hidden, alongside implicit understandings about mutual but informal rewards, incentives and reciprocities, and is distinguished from a 'prestige' economy (Blackmore and Kandiko 2012) and a 'gift' economy (Macfarlane 2015) by the expectation of reciprocity as a result of building social capital. Another example is the fact that some individuals having teaching-only contracts undertake research in their own time, either unfunded or locally funded, and research-only faculty undertake some teaching to build their portfolio, with the tacit agreement of local managers and colleagues who might perceive advantage in this for the department. These activities might well not feature in a formal annual review, but could be used in a curriculum vitae for future advancement. The notion of investment also comes into play, on a spectrum of being calculated or speculative, within relationships that may be open-ended on the basis of ongoing reciprocity, or restricted to a specific area of interest. Thus although such relationships may be facilitative and mutually beneficial, they may also acquire a perceived value based on, for instance, the prestige and visibility associated with the relationship, and exchange value in relation to the 'gift' of an opportunity such as attendance at a conference. Discretionary and voluntary relationships might therefore be said to represent part of a hidden, 'soft' economy on which institutions increasingly depend.

Building on the idea of *obligatory, discretionary* and *voluntary* relationships, it is possible to identify approaches that are *instrumental* or *investing*, either at an institutional or individual level. These are summarised in Table 8.2.

Instrumental relationships involve a clear *quid pro quo* with pre-defined outcomes and rewards, likely to be reflected in contractual agreements. In the case of individuals, they may involve meeting obligations with good enough performance, for instance restricting the amount of teaching undertaken in order to focus on achieving excellent research if this is seen as more likely to lead to career progression, thus fulfilling the requirements of a workload model but not going the extra mile with students. In relation to institutions, *instrumental* relationships are likely to lead to transactional partnerships that get the job done as efficiently as possible in areas of activity which are seen as discrete and clear cut. They are therefore likely to be measured and calculated. Such relationships are reflected in, for instance, outsourcing and the adoption of a private sector approach. However, it may also be that increasing numbers of part-time staff on teaching focused contracts may engender relationships that tend to be at the instrumental rather than investing end of the spectrum.

Investing relationships are likely to require trust, negotiation and indeed some faith. For the individual this may mean taking opportunities when it is not always clear what they may lead to, and for institutions it may mean taking a chance on

Table 8.2 Instrumental and investing relationships

Institutional/instrumental	Institutional/investing
Contracts of employment	Flexible employment packages
Workload models	Community partnerships and networks
Transactional arrangements e.g. shared services/outsourcing contracts	Developmental activity (mentoring, conferences, attachments …)
Individual/instrumental	**Individual/investing**
Fulfilling obligations	Working outside formal hours
'Good enough'/satisfactory performance	Focus on activities of intrinsic interest
Focus on activities likely to bring tangible reward such as funding	and/or involving innovation with uncertain outcomes
	Internal and external networking

initiatives and partnerships that may bring mutual benefits, which again cannot be predicted precisely. For both, networks are likely be built, extended and valued, a process that has been both facilitated and stimulated in contemporary environments by online relationships. For the individual, an investing relationship offers a degree of autonomy and freedom, for instance to seek new contacts and develop partnerships that might translate into funding and publications, and so is optimistic in tenor. In this sense they might be seen as being liberating and as adding value. There may also be a difference between team working that emerges voluntarily and as a matter of choice, and team working that is imposed, for instance by the merger of a department.

Linking back to the structural models of institutional approaches to managing faculty, described in Chapter 3, *investing* relationships would be more likely to occur in the *integrated* approach, with *instrumental* relationships more likely to characterise *private sector* approaches, and *partnership* approaches to engender a mix of the two, depending on the extent of pragmatic considerations, and of voluntarism in individual contributions. In general terms, more pliable policies and structures, for instance job descriptions that are not over-specific, are more likely to encourage *investing* relationships, although individual situations at any point in time are likely to involve a balance between the two. In turn, *investing* relationships may have an influence on policies and structures so that they become more facilitative. Nevertheless *instrumental* relationships are necessary to maintain contractual obligations on both sides, and also in relation to considerations of fairness and equity. Maintaining an appropriate balance offers a further perspective for managers on their portfolio of responsibilities.

Conclusion

The studies suggest that, whatever the shape or size of an institution, making policy work, and achieving desired outcomes of appropriate quality, is likely to depend on facilitative relationships day-to-day. In practice the segment of the institution that the individual inhabits, rather than the institution, may be the meaningful arena of activity. Thus as one respondent acknowledged:

> the culture is very consensual, very democratic and I feel very fortunate for that. It's not like that everywhere. (mid-career faculty)

Formal contractual arrangements such as pay and conditions, and informal understandings and expectations that contribute to the quality of the psychological contract, including a sense of recognition and opportunities for personal development, represent a critical relationship. Managing expectations on both sides, and the way in which institutional arrangements are interpreted by, for instance, heads of department and programme leaders, is likely to be paramount, for instance in balancing deteriorating staff student ratios with pressure on individual workloads. The trick for local managers is to recognise the interplay of policy and institutional structures with the agency of individuals and what they might achieve individually. The possibilities may only be apparent at local level. In fact as a number of respondents in the studies suggested, it is for local managers not only to recognise, but also to create, discretionary space in which potentials can be developed and realised. In turn, it is for senior management teams to ensure that institutional policies are as far as possible informed by and congruent with local practice.

Thus, structures alone are unlikely to be sufficient to safeguard and promote the interests of people with a range of career backgrounds and trajectories, and there is a major role for managers, mentors and individuals in facilitating policy implementation across a spectrum of *obligatory, discretionary* and *voluntary* relationships. However, the studies also suggest that there can be a tendency to conservatism with respect to existing structures, which may take time and effort to change, even where there is a will to do so. There may therefore also be a calculation on the part of individuals as to the extent to which it may be helpful to subscribe to existing structures and processes for the time being. Relationships are likely to be adjusted across a spectrum of *instrumental* and *investing* approaches, in order to accommodate the ebb and flow of individual and institutional aspirations.

Chapter 9

Conclusions

From the studies there would appear to be increasing recognition among senior and middle managers in higher education institutions of the needs and aspirations of a broadening range of faculty. This has resulted in significant efforts being made, particularly at middle management level, to accommodate individual requirements. However, depending on the flexibility of structures and the influence of individuals, there remains potential for a gap, as well as a time lag, between formal institutional structures and processes and what happens, or is perceived to happen, day-to-day. Local interpretation is likely to be an increasingly significant element in creating a facilitative environment, even where structures have become more flexible. This is evident, for instance, in the UK Annual Workforce Survey (Times Higher 2016) which demonstrates that, despite increasing time and work pressures on academic faculty, individual stories demonstrate how a key variable is likely to be local cultures, so that:

> Staff are ... more likely than not to say that their university cares for the wellbeing of its workforce (49% agree that they do, against 36% who disagree). (Times Higher 2016: 7)

It is also noticeable in this survey that negative views tend to be around structural factors, such as inappropriate application of workload models and performance management criteria, and also factors associated with a more market-oriented environment. It is likely to be these types of factors that lead to negative perceptions of managers as a collective, which also surface in the Annual Workforce Survey. Structures can be perceived, according to circumstances, as more or less flexible, imposed by senior managers, or constructed as a result of consultation and 'community governance'. Furthermore, structural changes may be cumulative and effectively layered on top of one other rather than one change precisely replacing another, with the potential for lack of clarity about, for instance, promotion criteria. Local managers are likely to have an influence in managing such processes, thereby influencing perceptions at ground level. Academic faculty are also influenced by disciplinary perspectives, although new interdisciplinary and inter-professional identities are emerging, with a general diffusion and flattening of such relationships.

This concluding chapter will discuss developments arising from the interaction between structures and relationships as more broadly based constituencies, both internal and external to the university, are incorporated.

Intentions and practice

On the one hand, notwithstanding attempts to flex structures and processes, these are often perceived as having become harder-edged as institutions endeavour to cope with the pressures arising from more market-oriented and accountable environments. On the other hand, the internal reality of academic endeavour for individuals tends to be fluid and open-ended. This tension is clearly reflected in the following comment:

> we have an awful lot more bureaucracy now ... there are a lot more limitations on what we can do. Flexibility is being taken away from us and it's as if the university wants to be run more like an industrial company but ... that to me is not what universities have always been about ... universities should be generating thinking, creative, and that sort of thing, and that requires flexibility ... If you start imposing what you'd expect them to do ... then I think it takes that creativity away ... 'thinking time'... is sadly lacking now....
> (mid-career faculty)

The HEA study in particular pointed to increasing tension, and at times distance, between teaching and research activity, at both individual and institutional levels, evidenced by the priorities accorded to research and teaching and the approaches taken to each activity by individuals, including 'hidden' time spent on one or the other. There may be implicit rules and practices in relation to recognition of specific types of activity, and the possibility of moving between different types of contract. Individuals may adopt different strategies to negotiate local structures and processes, drawing on both formal and informal understandings and relationships. In turn, an iterative process develops as institutions respond via formal policies and local interpretation of these, for instance in the provision of professional development opportunities.

Despite efforts by institutions to introduce more flexible structures, and what would appear to be the best intentions of senior managers, mismatch can occur between such intentions and the way that they are experienced by individuals. There is therefore ongoing potential for dissonance between intrinsic motivations and what are perceived as institutional values. There is also the added complexity of a range of perceptions between different groups of faculty, for instance those who are more attuned to knowledge transfer and working closely with industry or in practice settings, as opposed to those working in arts or the more qualitative end of social science disciplines. This means that local solutions and approaches become even more significant, highlighting the role of middle managers in translating what is intended as flexibility into practice. As shown in Chapter 5, these managers are likely to be instrumental in developing a culture of support and encouragement, and at its most extreme, counteracting what one mid-career member of faculty, who obviously felt disenfranchised, described as a 'culture of fear'. Thus intentions and practice are likely to converge at the level of local managers.

On the one hand, there was evidence at the institutional level of good practice in acknowledging the views of rank-and-file faculty, and of developing a two-way dialogue in ways that would generate ideas:

> if you look at our strategies and policy statements and corporate plans ... you would find all the right things said in relation to 'people are our most important asset' and ... I don't think that's false in any sense ... we've conducted a couple of staff surveys at the institutional level ... as a temperature gauge to ... look at the mood of the institution by different staff groups ... and then try and follow-through on aspects of it ... I think colleagues have welcomed the opportunity to give their views on these kinds of matters. (pro-vice-chancellor, education)

This extended to involving early career faculty and professional staff in working groups and discussions about, for instance, progression and reward mechanisms:

> in my conversations with heads of school and my observations of young career academics ... I would positively seek out opportunities to involve some of those staff (including professional support staff, not just academic staff) in those developments because I think it's good to have their ideas and their approaches and their challenge ... but I would see that as part of their career development. (pro-vice-chancellor, education)

On the other hand, it was acknowledged (at another institution) that there could be a lack of transparency in bringing together institutional intentions and day-to-day activity:

> there's no link, no clear, strong link to the ambitions in the university strategy and what that means for the workforce. (director of human resources)

The need to close communication gaps was a common theme, and although individual managers articulated an intention to work towards an alignment of understandings, these could not be assured simply by realigning structures or co-locating offices, as in the following example:

> there is a need to get a synergy between what we do in HR around corporate learning and what they do in academic development ... the idea of bring-ing them together was to create that synergy but I think all it did was put two different cultures and departments in the same structure, but getting

a common agenda had not been achieved. And it's getting that common agenda, regardless of the structure, that's going to be important going forward.... (director of human resources)

Key challenges arising for institutions included establishing understandings about what is valued and giving recognition to this. Examples included acknowledgement of the effort made by individuals who went above the call of duty in making a difference to the lives of students or generating external income. Perhaps most frustrating of all was a lack of information about criteria for promotion, or dissonance between what was said and what appeared to happen, summed up by one respondent:

there's a real reticence to ... recognise or promote or whatever if it's not written down on a piece of paper ... we love to be bound by the rules that we set ourselves and that makes us all feel comfortable because it's kind of defensible ... and actually what we should be doing is, I think ... be a little bit more organic and being able to say, 'For us as a university right here, right now, that is really valuable and in order for us to retain that, or recognise it or whatever, we're going to promote, we're going to reward, we're going to recognise you for it'. (director of human resources)

As explained by this respondent, institutions tend to be bound by rules and procedures for the sake of equity, whereas a looser approach would depend on developing an understanding of the relationship between what the individual might have to offer and what the institution needs at any point in time. Although some individuals in some institutions were edging towards this, there was the sense that they were treading a delicate path, and that middle managers might need to be to encouraged to be more confident and proactive in this respect.

A need for understandings to be achieved at the interstices of institutional structures was illustrated by the following comment:

I think one word sums it up for me and that is 'fragmented' ... but within those constraints we work co-operatively and collaboratively to achieve the university's objectives ... So I think that is the glue that is missing in terms of bringing these disparate functional areas together and ensuring that they're aligned in terms of resources, purposes, timescales, to deliver on what the university needs. (pro-vice-chancellor, education)

This aspiration has become more pressing as institutions have become more complex and activities ripple through a range of roles, agendas and stakeholders. It is illustrated by a cross-boundary faculty role across employability, teaching and learning:

My current role really requires me to lead and be responsible for the development of employability initiatives across the university, to provide that strategic direction of where we're going and to look at the learning and teaching strategy and make sure that we're very well aligned in terms of initiatives and support that we're offering, to both students, staff, employers, and all those kind of wider stakeholders that are part of that employability agenda within higher education ... it's a shared ownership and shared partnership approach to making sure that all the decision-making and the protocol that supports it is agreed and supported by everyone that's involved. (mid-career faculty)

This also suggests that career and succession planning, which in one sense might be seen as a structural matter based on market demand for academic programmes, staff turnover and professional development, requires a nuanced approach that takes account of local talent and potential. This is particularly so for individuals moving into 'third space' projects such as employability, with account taken of experience that is unique and pathfinding, but does not necessarily fit precisely into preconceived requirements. This is likely to require in-depth understandings at school and department level, with bottom up input to institutional planning around the workforce 'map'. Achieving such outcomes is also likely to depend, at least in some measure, on the interpretive powers of local managers.

A stretching of time and space

Analysis of the narratives reflected an increasing disjunction of time and space in relation to work itself, which meant that, for instance, the use of hours as a measurement of workload was not only imprecise, but also did not necessarily represent the richness of individual inputs to teaching, research or other activities. Similarly, data about numbers of part-time faculty do not necessarily reflect the fact that some of these individuals may wish to remain in a practice setting for a proportion of their time. Nor do they take account of the synergy that such faculty can provide to the curriculum, which may be disproportionate to the number of hours that they work:

> We believe that we gain enormously from the input that we get from visiting lecturers. They come from the city, they come from the media, they come from the banking sector, they come from international relations, they come from marketing ... And they add a freshness and a modernity to the programmes, which our students appreciate.... (vice-chancellor)

Some individuals, from their own choice, worked on short-term contracts, for instance in a spin-out company, perhaps having part-time teaching in different institutions, and finding security in having multiple options:

> we've got good industry links, we get lots of sponsorship from industry, so it's a nice little team that we've got going ... I struggle to see my career developing at [the university of xxx] and it's there almost as a fallback option

if other things I'm working on don't work out ... and I've got no huge incentive to become institutionalised in a university.... (mid-career faculty)

In a less commercially-oriented context, others expressed themselves to be comfortable in part-time teaching roles, or in split teaching and learning support or administrative roles:

> [I feel] comfortable in the dual role [teaching and e-learning support], earning a reasonable living and managing to do some research ... I could see myself staying in this sort of 50:50 role for quite a long time I think ... not least because it synthesises with my academic role. (early career, teaching-only faculty)

Others were working in a similar way with professional bodies, standards agencies and national disciplinary bodies, and saw themselves as having portfolio careers, with equal commitment to the university and another locale. This could also be advantageous from an institutional point of view, and in certain circumstances allow backfilling to release individuals to undertake career enhancing projects outwith their regular responsibilities:

> We have a register ... and once people are on the register ... then we can very quickly draw from that register and use people in quite flexible ways ... it's a zero hours contract and there's all that baggage associated with that in the media, but it's fantastic because if there's people that you want to draw into the teaching conversation, you can ... get them in teaching less than ten hours ... so if you have a member of staff that says, 'I've got an opportunity to go and do a secondment in Australia' or whatever, they can go away and do that and ... you can pick someone off the register and that works really well in terms of, I think, getting people in who can have interesting conversations, seeing how they work, seeing how they fit ... then hopefully they can get more and more involved. (mid-career faculty, programme leader)

Although an increase in short-term contracts has been seen by commentators in a negative light because of the lack of security they offer to individuals, and the fact that they could lead to a further casualisation of teaching and impact negatively on the student experience, it was also pointed out that such appointments provided some individuals with experience and opportunities that eventually put them in a stronger position to gain a permanent post:

> I think there's sometimes a double-edged sword to it, frankly ... one of the other barriers now, is that now that the Funding Councils have moved to what they would call 'bigger and more prestigious' awards, there's actually probably less of them to go around, less buy-outs, less temporary posts and I know one of the issues is the lack of progression, but actually without those staging posts ... my fear is that there's less opportunities now. (mid-career faculty)

Thus, 'casual' work and short-term appointments could provide stepping stones on the way to a permanent lectureship, despite their insecurity. Individuals needed to establish a research record to obtain a permanent job and were unable to do this without short-term funding. Often transition from one to another depended on contacts, or in some cases, what one person described as 'patronage'.

At the same time, definitions of research and scholarship were becoming more fluid, demonstrating how understandings of academic activity can be stretched:

> 'Scholarship', for me, the way I understand it, is a fluid concept that you can feed in whatever you want. So, for example, research could also be scholarship – so I told my head of school, for example, 'I have a lot of unpublished material that I want to write up and send to journalists and stuff, can that be my contribution to scholarship?', he said, 'Yeah, yeah, yeah, okay' but if this finishes, I might ... direct my scholarship efforts into something else; like nowadays they also give teaching grants, so maybe you can get a teaching grant and develop a curriculum for a specific programme ... you can make a case and say, 'Okay, I want my scholarship time to be used for something like this', and if your head of school is a person that wants to help you and accommodate different needs, they would allow you to do something like that. (early career, teaching-only faculty)

Similarly, one mid-career researcher saw what they were doing very much in terms of project management:

> I think ... 5% [of the role] is what I'm actually finding out ... doing my research into things, and then probably up to ... 50% is probably what I would call 'operational activities', so this is things like wanting to find things out that are not necessarily going to turn up new research papers straightaway, and then about half the time is the actual management of the different projects or organising meetings, managing documents, document control and those sorts of activities. (mid-career, research-only faculty)

Although this may have been a one-off case, it may be that different levels of administration and management are implicit in many teaching and research roles and are not necessarily recognised or rewarded. In turn, a number of programme leaders complained about the amount of 'administration' required. This could lead to the sense that those on teaching and research contracts, in particular those with ambition, were expected to undertake a portfolio of activity with an overwhelming range:

> I do find that the demands of the job are so various. As teaching or research academics you are expected to be really great at presentations, good at your teaching, excellent, you know, international world-leading

research, you're expected to be presenting at conferences, being invited
to do research seminars, but you are also expected to be really good at
publicity and public relations and selling the University at open days and
writing publicity ... Now we're being asked about knowledge exchange
and impact, so many different jobs which you don't get any training for at
all. (mid-career faculty)

Thus it would seem that working time, space and relationships are expanding
even as institutions seek to define and codify them more explicitly. A relatively
straightforward example is that individuals are expected to be able to multi-task,
and in the following case, multi-manage:

There's possibly something there that institutions maybe need to think
about in terms of sort of mid-career support to academics who find themselves playing different roles [e.g. programme director, director of graduate
studies] ... suddenly it's kind of managing time split between two different
line managers and things like that.... (mid-career faculty)

In a broader context, the increasing use made of the Internet and Skype for
communication has led to a further stretching of time and space. A number of
managers mentioned that staff tend to live at a greater distance geographically
from their institutions these days, often because of partner or family considerations, and that working from home is increasingly common, subject to individuals
being contactable during working hours. Relationships are also being stretched
by the use of blogs and social media, public and community engagement, and
multi-professional team environments. It can be debated whether relationships
between institutions and their employees are more or less stable as a result, but
a majority of managers felt that this kind of flexibility was part of contemporary
working life, that it engendered commitment from and between colleagues, and
that to contest it would have a disproportionately negative effect. It might also be
said that the concept of management is being stretched in that it is increasingly
seen as an ongoing process, rooted in relationships, as well as a discrete activity in
relation to decisions about specific issues.

One vice-chancellor spoke of holding a series of lunches with different categories of staff to talk about their work and what they saw as problematic in gaining
promotion, and to make early career staff feel that they had a presence and a
voice in the institution. At another institution anyone was free to communicate
directly with members of the senior management team without going through
a line manager, and regular all-staff meetings allowed everyone an opportunity
to 'ask and influence'. Such relationships seemed to have a ripple effect with
broader and longer-term impacts, in a way that restructuring alone could not
do. Middle managers in particular might be said to be creating, as well as
extending, space and time, in ways that offer more discretion to individuals and
also generate synergy.

The shape and size of an institution, or sub-unit within the institution, and the length and lateral reach of lines of communication, appeared to be significant variables in the formation of relationships. Thus:

> In xxx I had coffee with my dean every day, I had coffee with the vice-principal there once a week at least, we'd talk regularly, it was a much smaller institution, the lines of communication were smaller. Here, beyond my line manager, until more recently, there was no reason, you know, you had to follow the protocols.... (late career faculty)

> I think if you're one institution on one site, it can be a lot easier to implement your policies, we're a unitary institution but it's almost like federal in terms of the campuses. (pro-vice-chancellor, education)

This applied whatever the age, type and mission of the institution, although it could be influenced by the extent of devolved management and partnership arrangements, and the fact that individuals in applied disciplines were more likely to have external contacts and networks. Although it would appear that smaller, more closely knit institutions, or sections of institutions, were more likely to offer facilitative relationships whereby individuals could more closely identify with policy, there were also examples of active steps being taken to shorten lines of communication by providing leadership at nodal points within larger structures:

> one of the things that's prized about the institution is the short line of governance, and that's really quite emblematic.... We've put in mechanisms ... a go-to point, a facilitating point ... a senior academic who is providing ... leadership academically within the faculties. (director of human resources)

Whatever the length of lines of communication, however, there would appear to be increasing recognition that lateral relationships provide essential feedback loops to inform collaboration and allow learning to take place. This may include bringing together different 'activity systems' and the introduction of new 'arte-facts' (Engeström 2001: 131), as shown in Chapter 6.

Creating discursive space

The power of positive and sustaining relationships was a theme that recurred among early and mid-career faculty, particularly in closing gaps between policy and practice. On the one hand, there could be a reluctance to depart from the letter of the law in relation to, for instance, promotions, in order to justify decisions, and on the other hand a desire to play to individual strengths. Resolving this tension was something that both senior management team members and local managers felt was a priority, and again implied a focus on promoting relationships in which individuals felt confident about discussing their futures. As one director of human resources commented:

> [if] you try and please everyone with everything all the time … it never works … no-one gets exactly what they want out of it, so you're wasting your time and effort … targeted stuff is more labour intensive and more difficult to do, but the results at the end of it will be better. (director of human resources)

However the 'targeted stuff' is likely to involve one-to-one discussions and negotiations, in an atmosphere of trust, so that individuals perceive that they have an opportunity to achieve their goals, though perhaps not in the precise manner and timescale that they had anticipated. This was facilitated by the creation of discursive space, particularly at local level.

Tacit understandings appeared to be quite widespread, giving rise to solutions that suited the specific circumstances of an individual or department. In practical terms this could be to the advantage of individual by matching opportunities to individual strengths. Thus one person found relative freedom in a role that involved work with a disciplinary body that bought out their time. Although their institution was happy with this arrangement, they spoke of a 'disconnect' because they were not entirely mainstream, but nevertheless the situation worked for both sides on the basis of implicit understandings, without questions needing to be asked:

> They know I'm doing [disciplinary body project] but they don't necessarily care about the details, as long as I'm doing what I'm being paid to do, and so I think there can be like a sort of disconnect in that they don't know what you're doing. (mid-career faculty)

Thus, local practices might be known about but not fully articulated in order to leave options open, and it could be that the more precise and documented policies become, the more discursive space is required in order to apply these policies, in which a range of individual aspirations can be explored. For instance, it cannot necessarily be assumed that all individuals aspire to a teaching and research role:

> a lot of my friends are on 'either/or' contracts. I think the positive of it means that there's a clear progression route. If you are very teaching focused, there is a progression into the higher job roles, which perhaps wasn't that transparent … I think some people are very happy being on a teaching-only contract, and again, I think others would be very happy on a research-focused contract. (early career faculty)

This contrasts with a less pragmatic view, for instance, that:

> Increasingly I'm seeing posts that say 'teaching only' but that I don't see as a positive development because what they're saying is, 'Your workload plan will be filled with lots of teaching, we're not going to give you much time

or support for doing research.' And I don't know a single academic who doesn't want to do some research. (mid-career faculty)

A more sanguine view utilised understandings developed within a more discursive environment:

> the college view and the head of department's view is that I should be focusing on pedagogic development activities ... the long term view of my senior colleagues in my research group is that I need to get involved in research ... but it's not a strong conflict because I think everyone's very pragmatic and they know ... that ultimately I was going to end up doing your typical teaching and research mix, so I don't think anyone's particularly opposed to that. (early career, teaching-only faculty)

However, if not used sensitively, tacit understandings could lead to a sense of inequity, or uncertainty about, for instance, how to progress a career. Thus a programme leader found that what 'worked' for her was having an informal understanding with her line manager that she had a lower teaching load because of her management responsibilities, as a result of which 'he sees output' and she had found a niche for herself. However she acknowledged that the downside of such informal understandings could be that individuals could be 'politically wily and have informal deals with the boss'. Tacit assumptions could also include an expectation of voluntarism, whereby academic activity encroaches on what might be expected to be non-working hours. It was therefore a delicate balance, of which both local managers and rank-and-file faculty seemed to be aware. The extent to which discursive space extends beyond one-to-one discussions may be critical to the way that overall perceptions develop, for instance, an impression that teaching-only roles were emerging by default:

> We'd heard that discussions were going on in the departments but there are definitely now people around who are on teaching-only contracts, and so it happened at some stage, but quite recently and very much under the covers. There wasn't a big statement that people were now one or the other or a combination. (mid-career academic developer)

It would therefore appear to be essential that discursive space is perceived as being open, as well as facilitating one-to-one discussions.

Therefore, in common with the findings of Bacon (2014), Bolden et al (2008) and Jameson (2012) in relation to decision making that may take place more effectively outwith formal arenas, the studies suggest that implicit understandings are at times more powerful in enabling individual aspirations than those that are more explicit. The relationships underpinning understandings might be seen as existing in the space between 'collegiality' and 'managerialism', increasingly regarded as a false dichotomy (see for instance Tight 2014). This is particularly so in complex environments characterised by multiple and shifting variables, so that what is appropriate under one set of conditions may not be so in another. Thus, the creation of discursive space, in which individuals feel they can have an influence, emerges from the studies as a critical element of facilitative relationships.

Looking ahead

For the future, universities are now so complex that they might be regarded as similar in structure to multi-national companies, so that:

> there will be more creativity in ... contractual structures in the future ... a lot of change will creep in ... [with] more mergers in the higher education sector, more alliances, and as a prelude to that, more collaboration ... that will lead to not really just having a single university. (chair of council)

More flexible models and processes are likely to be introduced as and when opportunities arise, and the development of relationships with multiple partners and colleagues will be increasingly significant.

In turn, Kleinman and Vallas (2001) and Jong (2005) note a convergence of practices from commercial research enterprises to the academic sector. As a result, universities become more like other employing organisations with academics perceived as knowledge workers, so that university research may become less of a curiosity-driven activity and more like 'ordinary work ... with reputation and career opportunities linked to it' (Hendriks and Sousa 2008: 369). Conversely, private sector organisations may become more collegial with flatter, more networked structures so that:

> interdependent but isolated specialists are replaced by collective projects within which different specialists interact and work together for a period of time limited by the achievement of the mission for which they are gathered together ... [leading to] fading organisational careers (workers following the careers designed by internal markets in their firms) and the rise of boundary-less careers (workers being self-responsible for the construction and development of their individual careers). (Musselin 2007: 184)

Although governing body relationships were not a prime focus in either study, it was clear that some respondents saw scope for their members to take more of an interest in internal relationships. It seemed that although governors were interested in financial probity and general culture of the institution, there was a lacuna in relation to day-to-day interactions with faculty. As one vice-chancellor put it:

> If you were to do an analysis of governing body agendas, I think you'd hunt to find anything on HR ... they care about staff, about the staff contract,

the way in which you use staff, and they care about managing redundancies, restructurings, appropriately, but ... the way you use staff, I've never heard a discussion of that at governors. (vice-chancellor)

Thus, challenges remain. Management processes are required that allow for timely responses to external requirements as well as an appropriate iteration with faculty. Recognising the value and potential of new activities and roles is likely to involve a range of options that are not mutually exclusive, and could involve different models and relationships for different schools or departments. At the same time, individual aspirations may require careful negotiation vis-a-vis equity and fairness. This need not imply absolute equivalence across the board, as long as there are criteria that guide exceptions to the norm but allow for local variation. This demonstrates that flexibility works both ways, and is part of the ongoing relationship that characterises the psychological contract.

Some institutions are more proactive than others in looking at ways in which they might develop the potential of individuals, whose roles may vary significantly in relation to both the content of their work and the employment contract (Locke, Whitchurch et al 2016). This can lead to a situation in which changes happen in an *ad hoc* way, so that individuals are to a greater or lesser extent thrown back on their own resources in planning their futures. There may be a time lag before institutions integrate their human resource and staff development policies with institutional strategy as a whole, and a resulting tension between individuals feeling '"masters of their fate" as opposed to corporate employees subject to institutional administrative action' (Finkelstein 2015: 326). Achieving a match between individual pathways and collective profiles in departments and schools is likely to require facilitative structures and local relationships that promote 'holistic alignment between systemic, institutional and individual drivers and performance' (Bentley et al 2015: 311).

Concluding remarks

From the studies, there would appear to be increased awareness among local managers of a mixed economy of activities that is sensitive to individual aspirations and potential opportunities, whilst coping with uncertainty and changing policy environments. This is likely to involve bridging formal and explicit agendas with tacit understandings, and accepting that there may be a time lag before structural changes, such as adjustments to career tracks or promotion criteria, can be accommodated. Moreover, as one vice-chancellor commented, 'there's some flexibility costs you more than the benefits you get'. This cost–benefit analysis involves weighing 'hard' and 'soft' benefits, including goodwill, and assessing how far boundaries can be pushed. This equation could be said to be at the heart of working relationships. Managing it may well fall to local managers such as heads of school and department, and include interpreting employment models in ways that inspire confidence, as well as maintaining the motivation and morale of individuals. Moderation of staffing models, therefore, is likely to continue to evolve. Individuals in higher education may increasingly have some type of portfolio career, mirroring models of work emerging from knowledge-based industries, including periods of time outside higher education. This may involve a shift towards non-positional careers, with loyalty to projects, and the prime task of 'management' being the co-ordination of teams and networks and the building of relationships (Middlehurst 2010b). Furthermore, the studies showed very clearly that processes of institutional transition and evolution are ongoing, and that relationships are more likely to respond and adapt to contextual variables, at least in the short term, than structures.

Thus while institutions have taken steps at a structural level to achieve greater flexibility, designing a new system or adapting an old one to deal with emergent needs or problems is only half the story. It is also likely to require a discursive approach that is responsive to the aspirations and initiatives of individuals and builds on these. An emphasis on the importance of relationships in developing positive cultures and constructive attitudes was pervasive, and something that middle managers particularly sought to establish:

> I suppose I'm always more interested in culture than strategy … because I think strategy can come and go and actually none of us know what will happen in the future. So often, good outcomes emerge from the right culture … the right behaviour, interpersonal behaviour … we're still not properly respecting and supporting those people who, for example, very admirable people who are quite happy to remain as a grade 6 un-promoted lecturer and do an excellent job in that, but feel for various reasons that they're not supported or respected in that. (late career, teaching-only faculty)

Structures are undoubtedly necessary and valuable to ensure probity and equity, as evidenced in the desire of trade unions for adherence to terms and conditions that they have negotiated. In contemporary environments, however, such structures might be seen as a default position, and the ways in which they are applied may ultimately be more significant than the fact that they are in place. For instance, there was evidence that in some settings early career faculty saw formal requirements such as annual review as an opportunity for dialogue and feedback, rather than as a threat aligned with performance management. Thus:

> Whilst you can see it as a control mechanism, there's lots of young staff say to me, I want this because I want to know how I can get promoted. I want to know how well I've done … It's instructive in itself, who sees it as negative and who sees it as positive. (head of school)

This type of response was likely to depend on the creation of a safe environment for discussion, as well as the separation of career development from appraisal mechanisms. It was also likely to depend on what one senior manager described as 'mature relationships' that permit 'grown-up conversations', in which priorities on both sides can be articulated. This sense of a mutual discussion in which both individual and institution can benefit was one that recurred:

> we should all be talking as a school about how we should proceed and as a [university] how we should proceed as well ... I'd like to see [the university] communicating with itself better.... (early career faculty)

Because universities are increasingly diverse communities, relationships are formed with fellow professionals internally and externally. These relationships might be described as the kindling that ignites the activity needed to drive agendas forward. Thus, rather than simply being a conduit for information to flow, they also stimulate action. On the one hand, when relationships work well, they can have a powerful effect on the flow of a career. On the other hand, if relationships are missing or exist only on paper, this can lead to an absence or deficit, of which the individual may or may not be aware. This in turn can lead to a sense of isolation, a questioning of purpose and demotivation.

Thus, relationships can help to open up new spaces and unlock futures, for instance triggering an individual's involvement in a specific project, or giving an individual local responsibilities and the opportunity to build and lead a team. One senior manager referred to developing 'spatial and temporal flexibility' so that individuals could undertake activity across different areas of interest at different times in their career. This kind of approach offered 'a more fluid, kind of organic way of recognising what's important for the university at [any] moment in time'. Relationships, therefore, may have a disproportionate effect, both positively and negatively, and be more than the sum of their parts, whereas structural imperatives tend to focus on linear and temporal understandings and outcomes. This echoes Engeström's findings in relation to people-centred activity in health care settings:

> Fundamentally, both care relationships and critical paths are linear and temporal constructions of the object. They have great difficulties in representing and guiding horizontal and socio-spatial relations and interactions between care providers located in different institutions, including the patient and his/her family as the most important actors in care. (Engeström 2005b: 73)

Thus, even in progression schemes that recognise the possibility of different career tracks, something more fine-tuned is likely to be needed. A breaking down of the mono-contract and salary scale, and unpacking of structures based on identical terms and conditions for all, is something that higher education institutions in more market-oriented environments are grappling with, wishing to maintain the principle of equity, but not necessarily homogeneity. This may include a variety of incentives in the employment package that may be attractive in different ways to different segments of the workforce. Judgements need to be made both by institutions and individuals about the balance of risk in relation to levels of longer-term security, and some individuals who find it difficult to obtain a permanent post might leave the system. For such reasons, one respondent felt that it was important for employability initiatives to be incorporated into doctoral programmes, geared to opportunities within academia but also in adjacent professions, business and industry, depending on the discipline. Building positive relationships on the part of line managers, therefore, is likely to involve playing to strength and providing a reasonable sense of security, and on the part of individuals, making fine judgements about the risks involved in taking on new or innovative activity.

Inevitably, a challenging of agendas, whether bottom up or top down, can at times lead to resistance, but such pushback can also stimulate an iterative process around the appropriateness and value of new practices. The studies illustrate that whereas organisational structures may take time to change, day-to-day relationships tend to be more fluid, less time constrained, and more mobile, allowing boundaries to be tested and adjustments to be made on an ongoing basis. Although this may suit those who are active in developing support networks and influencing key decision makers, care is also needed to ensure that those who are less resilient or confident have the opportunity to have their voices heard. Recognition of the significance of local, dialogic relationships also suggests a shift for managers from solving boundary disputes between individuals and departments towards a more holistic approach to developing collective interests and identities. This sense of a two-way process was summed up by one director of human resources:

> It's managing that constant message that you're at a place that's going places, and that you're engaged in stuff that's interesting and exciting and ... as well as the monetary side of things ... It's about feeling that you're connected and you belong ... You have to manage that eclectically because you know each department has a slightly different way of doing things, it's own norms ... and the university is some kind of faceless concept.... (director of human resources)

In responding to external agendas, and also pressure from staff themselves, institutions are experimenting with new practices whilst trying sustain and develop existing ones. It would appear that a premium is increasingly placed on communicative relationships and that these contribute to the social and intellectual capital of institutions. They are likely to require investment by faculty, and may in turn translate into new forms of collegial governance, bringing together 'external [institutional] image' and 'internal meaning and value' (Henkel 2016: 219). Local managers such as heads of department have an important role to play in managing this process, which includes interpreting formal contracts, supporting institutional aspirations, and assessing at what point arrangements might be optimal for individuals as well as for their department or school. This in turn may stimulate:

> more individuals [being] willing to adapt and make new choices and modes of working in the task of helping their institutions to keep pace with the changes confronting them. (Henkel 2016: 220)

Local managers, therefore, should be supported in working constructively with academic faculty in local settings, where necessary on a case-by-case basis, so that faculty feel fully recognised and authenticated in their roles. It would also appear that small adjustments, whether formal or informal, and whether perceived as positive or negative, can have a disproportionate effect. Whilst greater fluidity seems likely to continue to challenge institutional policy-making, it does not diminish the need to ensure that staff find it attractive, motivating and rewarding to work in a higher education institution, and that what institutions offer in most respects meets their expectations. Institutions will therefore wish to consider some of the challenges outlined in this volume, weighing the balance of advantage of new practices with the range of options available.

References

Altbach, P., (Ed.). (1996). *The International Academic Profession: A Special Report*. Princeton, NJ: Carnegie Foundation for the Advancement of Learning.

Anderson, V. (2007). "Contingent and marginalized? Academic development and part-time teachers." *International Journal for Academic Development* 12(2): 111–121.

Angervall, P. and J. Gustafsson (2015). "Invited to academia. Recruited for science or teaching in Education Sciences." *Scandinavian Journal of Educational Research*. DOI: http://dx.doi.org/10.1080/00313831.2015.1066432.

Archer, L. (2008). "Younger academics' constructions of 'authenticity', 'success' and professional identity." *Studies in Higher Education* 33(4): 385–403.

Archer, W. (2005). *Mission Critical? Modernising Human Resource Management in Higher Education*. Oxford: Higher Education Policy Institute.

Austin, A. (2010). Expectations and Experiences of Early Career Academics. In *Becoming an Academic*. Eds. L. McAlpine and G. Akerlind. Basingstoke: Palgrave Macmillan, 18–44.

Australian Learning and Teaching Council (ALTC) (2008). *The RED Report: Recognition, Enhancement, Development*. Sydney: ALTC.

Bacon, E. (2014) *Neo-Collegiality: Restoring Academic Engagement in the Managerial University*. London: The Leadership Foundation for Higher Education.

Ball, S. (2008). "New philanthropy, new networks and new goverance in education." *Political Studies* 56(4): 744–765.

Barrett, P. and L. Barrett (2006). "Balancing workloads: A timely issue." *In Practice*. London: Leadership Foundation for Higher Education.

Barrett, P. and L. Barrett (2007). "Current practice in the allocation of academic workloads." *Higher Education Quarterly* 61: 461–478.

Barrett, P. and L. Barrett (2010). "Cycles of innovation in managing academic workloads." *Higher Education Quarterly* 64(2): 183–199.

Baxter, J. (2010). *Bien dans sa Peau? An investigation into the role of professional learning in the formation of online teaching identities of part-time academics*. Academic Identities in the Twenty-First Century, University of Strathclyde 16–18 June 2010.

Benington, J. (2011). From Private Choice to Public Value? In *Public Value: Theory and Practice*. Eds. J. Bennington and M. Moore. Basingstoke: Palgrave Macmillan, 31–51.

Bentley, P., H. Coates, I. Dobson, L. Goedegebuure and V. L. Meek (2015). Academic Job Satisfaction from an International, Comparative Perspective.

In *Forming, Recruiting and Managing the Academic Profession*. Eds. U. Teichler and W. K. Cummings. Dordrecht: Springer, 187–209.

Bexley, W., R. James, and S. Arkoudis (2011). *The Australian Academic Profession in Transition: Addressing the Challenge of Reconceptualising Academic Work and Regenerating the Academic Workforce*. Melbourne: Centre for the Study of Higher Education.

Biggs, J. (1996). "Enhancing teaching through constructive alignment." *Higher Education* 32: 347–364.

Blackmore, P. and C. Kandiko (2012). "Academic motivation: Exploring prestige economies." *In Practice* 28: 1–4. London: Leadership Foundation for Higher Education.

Blackmore, P. (2016). *Prestige in Academic Life: Excellence and Exclusion*. New York: Routledge.

Blass, E., A. Jasman, and S. Shelley (2010). *The Future of Higher Education Provision in the UK: Workforce Implications. A Review of the Literature. A Report to HEFCE*. Bristol: HEFCE.

Bolden, R., G. Petrov and J. Gosling (2008) *Developing Collective Leadership in Higher Education*. London: Leadership Foundation for Higher Education.

Bolden, R., S. Jones, H. Davis and P. Gentle (2015). *Developing and Sustaining Shared Leadership in Higher Education*. London: Leadership Foundation for Higher Education.

Boon, S. (2010). Finding the path, walking the path: Educational development as professional journey. In *Creating a Profession: Building Careers in Educational Development*. Eds. S. Boon, B. Matthew and L. Sheward. SEDA Special Publication 27.

Bourdieu, P. (1988). *Homo Academicus*. Cambridge: Polity Press.

Bourdieu, P. (1993). *The Field of Cultural Production*. Cambridge: Polity Press.

Bourdieu, P. and L. J. D. Wacquant (1992). *An Invitation to Reflexive Sociology*. Chicago and London: University of Chicago Press.

Boyer, E. L. (1990). *Scholarship Reconsidered: Priorities for the Professoriate*. Princeton, NJ: Carnegie Foundation for the Advancement of Teaching.

Boyer, E. L., P.G. Altbach and M. J. Whitelaw (1994). *The Academic Profession. An International Perspective*. Princeton, NJ: Carnegie Foundation for the Advancement of Teaching.

Branson, C., M. Franken and D. Penney (2016). "Middle leadership in higher education: A relational analysis." *Educational Management Administration and Leadership* 44(1): 128–145.

Braun, V. and Clarke, V. (2013). *Successful Qualitative Research: A Practical Guide for Beginners*. London: Sage.

Brechelmacher, A., E. Park, G. Ates and D. Campbell (2015). The Rocky Road to Tenure – Career Paths in Academia. In *Academic Work and Careers in Europe: Trends, Challenges, Perspectives*. Eds. T. Fumasoli, G. Goastellec and B. Kehm. Dordrecht: Springer, 13–40.

Brennan, J., W. Locke and R. Naidoo (2007). United Kingdom: An Increasingly Differentiated Profession. In *The Changing Conditions for Academic Work and Careers in Select Countries*. Eds. W. Locke and U. Teichler. Kassel: INCHER-Kassel, 163–176.

Brown, D. and M. Gold (2007). "Academics on non-standard contracts in UK universities: Portfolio work, choice and consumption." *Higher Education Quarterly* 61(4): 439–460.

Brown, R. and H. Carasso (2013). *Everything for Sale? The Marketisation of UK Higher Education*. New York: Routledge.

Bryson, C. (2004). *Strategic Approaches to Managing and Developing Part-Time Teachers: A Study of Five Higher Education Institutions*. York: LTSN Generic Centre.

Bryson, C. and R. Blackwell (2006). "Managing temporary workers in higher education: still at the margin?" *Personnel Review* 35(2): 207–224.

Cahill, J., J. Bowyer, C. Rendell, A. Hammond and S. Korek (2015). "An exploration of how programme leaders in higher education can be prepared and supported to discharge their roles and responsibilities effectively." *Educational Research* 57(3): 272–286.

Callender, C. and P. Scott (Eds.) (2013). *Browne and Beyond: Modernizing English Higher Education*. Bedford Way Papers 42. London: IOE Press.

Cavalli, A. and R. Moscati (2010). "Academic systems and professional conditions in five European countries." *European Review* 18(Supplement 1): 35–53.

Chartered Institute of Personnel and Development (2008). *Managing Change. The Role of the Psychological Contract*. London: CIPD.

Chartered Institute of Personnel and Development (2011). *Rewards and Pay: An Overview*. London: CIPD. www.cipd.co.uk/hr-resources/factsheets/reward-pay-overview.aspx.

Clarke, M., A. Hyde and J. Drennan (2013). Professional Identity in Higher Education. In *The Academic Profession in Europe: New Tasks and New Challenges*. Eds. B. Kehm and U. Teichler. Dordrecht: Springer, 7–22.

Clarke, M. (2015). *Creating a Supportive Working Environment in European Higher Education*. Brussels: Education International Research Institute.

Clegg, S. and J. McAuley (2005). "Conceptualising middle management in higher education: A multifaceted discourse." *Journal of Higher Education Policy and Management* 27: 19–34.

Coaldrake, P. (2000). "Rethinking academic and university work." *Higher Education Management* 12(3): 7–30.

Coates, H. and L. Goedegebuure (2010). *The Real Academic Revolution*. Melbourne: L. H. Martin Institute.

Cook, C. and L. Daunton (2014). 'Human Resource Management' Implications of Working Lives Research. In *Academic Working Lives: Experience, Practice and Change*. Eds. L.Gornall, C. Cook, L. Daunton, J. Salisbury and B. Thomas. London: Bloomsbury, 271–279.

Crawford, C. (2012) *Socio-Economic Gaps in HE Participation: How Have They Changed over Time?* IFS Briefing Note BN133, London: Institute for Fiscal Studies.

Creswell, J. (1998). *Qualitative Inquiry and Research Design: Choosing Among Five Traditions*. Thousand Oaks, CA: Sage Publications.

Crosby, B. C. and J. M. Bryson (2010). "Integrative leadership and the creation and maintenance of cross-sector collaborations." *The Leadership Quarterly* 21(2): 211–230.

Csikszentmihalyi, M. (1990). *Flow: The Psychology of Optimal Experience*. New York: Harper and Row.

Cullinane, N. and T. Dundon (2006). "The psychological contract: A critical review." *International Journal of Management Review* 8(2): 113–129.

Cummings, W. and M. Finkelstein (2012). *Scholars in the Changing American Academy: New Contexts, New Rules and New Roles.* Dordrecht: Springer.

Davis, A., M. J. van Rensburg and P. Venter (2016). "The impact of managerialism on the strategy work of university middle managers." *Studies in Higher Education* 41(8): 1480–1494.

Deem, R., S. Hillyard and M. Reed (2007). *Knowledge, Higher Education, and the New Managerialism: The Changing Management of UK Universities.* Oxford: Oxford University Press.

Delanty, G. (2005). *Social Science: Philosophical and Methodological Foundations.* New York: Open University Press.

Delanty, G. (2008). Academic Identities and Institutional Change. In *Changing Identities in Higher Education: Voicing Perspectives.* Eds. R. Barnett and R. di Napoli. Abingdon: Routledge, 124–133.

Denis, J-L., E. Ferlie and N. Van Gestel (2015). "Understanding Hybridity in Public Organisations." *Public Administration* 93(2): 273–289.

Department for Business, Education and Skills (2011). *Putting Students at the Heart of Higher Education.* Cm 8122. Norwich, TSO. www.gov.uk/government/news/putting-students-at-the-heart-of-higher-education.

Department for Business, Education and Skills (2016). *Success as a Knowledge Economy. Teaching Excellence, Social Mobility and Student Choice.* London: Department for Business, Education and Skills.

Dowd, K. O. and Kaplan, D. M. (2005). "The career life of academics: Boundaried or boundaryless?" *Human Relations* 58(6): 699–721.

Duberley, J., L. Cohen and E. Leeson (2007). "Entrepreneurial academics: Developing scientific careers in changing university settings." *Higher Education Quarterly* 61(4): 479–497.

Engeström, Y. (1987). *Learning by Expanding: An Activity-Theoretical Approach to Developmental Research.* Helsinki: Orienta-Konsultit.

Engeström, Y. (2001). "Expansive learning at work: Toward an activity theoretical reconceptualization." *Journal of Education and Work* 14: 133–156.

Engeström, Y. (2005a) *Activity Theory and Expansive Design.* http:/projectsfinal. interactionivrea.org/2004-2005/SYMPOSIUM%202005communication%20 material/ACTIVITY%20THEORY%20AND%20EXPANSIV%20DESIGN_ Engestrom.pdf

Engeström, Y. (2005b). *Developmental Work Research. Expanding Activity Theory in Practice.* Berlin: International Cultural-historical Human Sciences.

EU (2008). Report of the Mission for Flexicurity. http://ec.europa.eu/social/Blob Servlet?docId=1515&langId=en

Fanghanel, J. (2012). *Being an Academic.* Abingdon, Routledge.

Feldman, M., and A. Khademian (2007). "The role of the public manager in inclusion: Creating communities of participation." *Governance: An International Journal of Policy, Administration and Institutions* 20(2): 305–324.

Ferlie, E., C. Musselin and G. Andresani (2008). "The steering of higher education systems: a public management perspective." *Higher Education* 56(3): 325–348.

Finkelstein, M. J. (2007). The 'New' Look of Academic Careers in the United States. In *Key Challenges to the Academic Profession.* Eds. M. Kogan and U. Teichler. Kassel, Germany. UNESCO Forum on Higher Education and International Centre for Higher Education and Research, 145–158.

Finkelstein, M. (2009). Changing Employment Relations in North America: Academic Work in the United States, Canada and Mexico. In *The Changing Face of Academic Life: Analytical and Comparative Perspectives*. Eds. J. Enders and E. de Weert. Basingstoke: Palgrave Macmillan, 218–247.

Finkelstein, M. (2010). "Diversification in the academic workforce: The case of the US and implications for Europe." *European Review* 18(1): 141–156.

Finkelstein, M. (2015). How National Contexts Shape Academic Careers: A Preliminary Analysis. In *Forming, Recruiting and Managing the Academic Profession*. Eds. U. Teichler and W. K. Cummings. Dordrecht: Springer, 317–328.

Florida, R. (2002). *The Rise of the Creative Class*. New York: Basic Books.

Floyd, A. (2015). "Supporting academic middle managers in higher education: Do we care?" *Higher Education Policy* 29(2): 167–183.

Fumasoli, T., G. Goastellec and B. Kehm (2015). Academic Careers and Work in Europe: Trends, Challenges, Perspectives. In *Academic Work and Careers in Europe: Trends, Challenges, Perspectives*. Eds. T. Fumasoli, G. Goastellec and B. Kehm. Dordrecht: Springer, 201–214.

Fumasoli, T. (2015). Strategic Management of Academic Human Resources: A Comparative Analysis of Flagship Universities in Norway, Finland, Switzerland and Austria. In *New Voices in Higher Education Research and Scholarship*. Eds. F. Ribeiro, Y. Politis and B. Culum. Hershey, PA: IGI Global, 18–37.

Galison, P. (1997). *Image and Logic: A Material Culture of Microphysics*. Chicago: The University of Chicago Press.

Gordon, G. (2003). "University roles and career paths: Trends, scenarios and motivational challenges." *Higher Education Management and Policy* 15(3): 89–103.

Gordon, G. and C. Whitchurch (Eds.) (2010). *Academic and Professional Identities in Higher Education: The Challenges of a Diversifying Workforce*. International Studies in Higher Education. New York: Routledge.

Gosling, D. (2009). "Educational development in the UK: A complex and contradictory reality." *International Journal for Academic Development* 14(1): 5–18.

Gourlay, L. and D. Sabri (2010). *Where Is the Knowledge in the Wisdom of Practice? Locating Academic Expertise in Professional Disciplines*. SRHE Conference 14–16 December 2010, Newport.

Granovetter, M. (1973) "The strength of weak ties." *American Journal of Sociology* 78(6): 1360–1380.

Guest, D. and M. Clinton (2007). *Human Resource Management and University Performance*. London: Leadership Foundation for Higher Education.

Hall, A. (2009). *Getting to Grips with Human Resource Management. Resources for Governors of UK Universities and Higher Education Colleges*. London: Leadership Foundation for Higher Education/Committee of University Chairs.

Hellawell, D. and N. Hancock (2001). "A case study of the changing role of the academic middle manager in higher education: between hierarchical control and collegiality?" *Research Papers in Education* 16(2): 183–197.

Hendriks, P. and Sousa, C. (2008). "Motivating university researchers." *Higher Education Policy* 21: 359–376.

Henkel, M. (2007). Shifting Boundaries and the Academic Profession. In *Key Challenges to the Academic Profession*. Eds. M. Kogan and U. Teichler. Paris and Kassel: International Centre for Higher Education Research Kassel, 191–204.

Henkel, M. (2012). Exploring New Academic Identities in Turbulent Times. In *Managing Reform in Universities: The Dynamics of Culture, Identity and Organisational Change*. Eds. B. Stensaker, J. Valimaa and C. Sarrico. Basingstoke: Palgrave Macmillan, 156–176.

Henkel, M. (2016). Multiversities and Academic Identities: Change, Continuities, and Complexities. In *Organising Academic Work in Higher Education: Teaching, Learning and Academic Identities*. Eds. L. Leisyte and U. Wilkesmann. New York: Routledge, 205–222.

Higher Education Academy (HEA) (2009). *Supporting Part-Time Teaching Staff in Higher Education within the Fields of Business, Management, Accountancy and Finance; and Health Sciences & Practice*. http://www.heacademy.ac.uk/business/projects/detail/Supporting_Part-Time_Teaching_Staff_in_HE.

Higher Education Funding Council for England (HEFCE) (Dowds) (2009a). *International Experiences of Human Resource Management in Higher Education*. Bristol: HEFCE.

Higher Education Funding Council for England (HEFCE) (Oakleigh Consulting) (2009b). *Evaluation of the Impact of Public Policy and Investments in Human Resource Management in Higher Education since 2001*. Bristol: HEFCE.

Higher Education Funding Council for England (Public and Corporate Economic Consultants/Centre for Business Research (PACEC/CBR)) (2009c). *Evaluation of the Effectiveness and Role of HEFCE/OSI Third Stream Funding: A Report to HEFCE by PACEC and the CBR*. Bristol: HEFCE.

Higher Education Funding Council for England (HEFCE) (PA Consulting) (2010). *The Future Workforce for Higher Education*. Overview Report. Bristol: HEFCE.

Higher Education Funding Council for England (HEFCE) (2012). *Collaborations, Alliances and Mergers in Higher Education: Consultation on Lessons Learned and Guidance for Institutions*. Bristol: HEFCE.

Higher Education Funding Council for England (HEFCE) (2014) *REF 2014 – Key Facts Leaflet*. Bristol: HEFCE.

Higher Education Statistics Agency (HESA) (2015). *Resources of Higher Education Institutions 2013–2014*. Cheltenham: HESA.

Higher Education Statistics Agency (HESA) (2016). *Resources of Higher Education Institutions 2014–2015*. Cheltenham: HESA.

Hirsch, W. and C. Jackson (2004). *Managing Careers in Large Organisations*. London: The Work Foundation.

Hogg, M., D. van Knippenberg and D. Rast (2012). "Intergroup leadership in organizations: Leading across group and organizational boundaries." *Academy of Management Review* (37)2: 232–255.

Holbeche, L. (2012). *Changing times in UK universities: What difference can HR make?* UniversitiesHR. http://www.uhr.ac.uk/uploadedfiles/Documents/Changing%20times%20in%20UK%20universities%20%28print%20version%29.pdf.

Huisman, J. (Ed.) (2009). *International Perspectives on the Governance of Higher Education: Alternative Frameworks of Co-ordination*. London: Routledge.

James, R. and E. Bare (2007). *Supporting Success and Productivity. Practical Tools for Making Your University a Great Place to Work*. OECD/IMHE "What Works" Conference, Paris, 3–4 September. www.oecd.org/edu/imhe/39190071.pdf.

Jameson, J. (2012) "Leadership values, trust and negative capability: Managing the uncertainties of future English higher education." *Higher Education Quarterly,* 66(4): 391–414.

Jones, G., J. Weinrib, A. Metcalfe, D. Fisher, K. Rubenson and I. Snee (2012). "Perceptions of early career faculty and the academic workplace in Canada." *Higher Education Quarterly* 66(2): 189–206.

Jong, S. (2005). *How Industry Ties Shape the Organization of Science; Reorganizations at Berkeley and Stanford after the Birth of the Biotech Industry.* European Forum on the Role of Universities in Innovation Systems, European University Institute, Florence, June.

Kallenberg, A. J. (2007). "Strategic innovation in higher education: The roles of academic middle managers." *Tertiary Education and Management* 13(1): 19–33.

Kehm, B. and U. Teichler (Eds.) (2012). *The Academic Profession in Europe: New Tasks and New Challenges.* Dordrecht: Springer.

Kinman, G. and S. Court (2010). "Psychosocial hazards in UK universities: Adopting a risk assessment approach." *Higher Education Quarterly* 64(4): 413–428.

Kleinman, D. L. and S. P. Vallas (2001). "Sciences, capitalism and the rise of the 'knowledge worker': The changing structure of knowledge production in the United States." *Theory and Society* 30(4): 451–492.

Knight, P., D. Baume, J. Tait and M. Yorke (2007). "Enhancing part-time teaching in higher education: A challenge for institutional policy and practice." *Higher Education Quarterly* 61(4): 420–438.

Kwiek, M. and D. Antonowicz, (2015). The Changing Paths in Academic Careers in European Universities: Minor Steps and Major Milestones. In *Academic Work and Careers in Europe: Trends, Challenges, Perspectives.* Eds. T. Fumasoli, G. Goastellec and B. Kehm. Dordrecht: Springer, 41–68.

Kyvik, S. (2009). "Allocating time resources for research between academic staff: The case of Norwegian university colleges." *Higher Education Management and Policy* 21(3): 109–122.

Land, R. (2010). Educational Developers: Identity in Paradox? In *Creating a Profession: Building Careers in Educational Development.* Eds. S. Boon, B. Matthew and L. Sheward. SEDA Special Publication 27.

Law, D. (2010). Changing Identities of Library and IS Staff. In *Academic and Professional Identities in Higher Education: The Challenges of a Diversifying Workforce.* Eds. G. Gordon and C. Whitchurch. New York, Routledge, 185–198.

Leisyte, L. (2016). Bridging the duality between universities and the academic profession: A tale of protected spaces, strategic gaming, and institutional entrepreneurs. In *Organising Academic Work in Higher Education: Teaching, Learning and Academic Identities.* Eds. L. Leisyte and U. Wilkesmann. New York: Routledge, 55–67.

Locke, W. (2014) *Shifting Academic Careers: Implications for Enhancing Professionalism in Teaching and Supporting Learning.* York: Higher Education Academy.

Locke, W. and A. Bennion (2010). *The Changing Academic Profession in the UK and Beyond.* Research Report for UniversitiesUK. London: UUK.

Locke, W. and A. Bennion (2011). The United Kingdom: Academic Retreat or Professional Renewal? In *Changing Governance and Management in Higher Education. The Perspectives of the Academy.* Eds. W. Locke, W. K. Cummings and D. Fisher. Dordrecht: Springer, 175–198.

Locke, W., W. K. Cummings and D. Fisher (Eds.) (2011). *Changing Governance and Management in Higher Education. The Perspectives of the Academy.* Dordrecht: Springer.

Locke, W., C. Whitchurch, H. Smith and A. Mazenod (2016). *Shifting Landscapes: meeting the staff development needs of the changing academic workforce.* York: Higher Education Academy.

Macfarlane, B. (2007a). *The Academic Citizen: The Virtue of Service in Academic Life.* New York: Routledge.

Macfarlane, B. (2007b). "Defining and rewarding academic citizenship: The implications for university promotions policy." *Journal of Higher Education Policy and Management* 29(3): 261–273.

Macfarlane, B. (2010). "The morphing of academic practice: Unbundling and the rise of the para-academic." *Higher Education Quarterly* 65(1): 59–73.

Macfarlane, B. (2015). "The ethics of multiple authorship: Power, performativity and the gift economy." *Studies in Higher Education.* DOI: 10.1080/030750 79.2015.1085009.

Malcolm, J. (2010). *Academic Workplace(s) and the Shaping of Academic Work.* SRHE Conference, 14–16 December 2010, Newport.

Marginson, S. (2013) "The impossibility of capitalist markets in higher education." *Journal of Education Policy* 28(3): 353–370.

Martin, E. (1999). *Changing Academic Work: Developing the Learning University.* Buckingham: SRHE/Open University Press.

McAlpine, L. (2010). *Meaning and Purpose in Academic Work: Implications for Early Career Academics.* SRHE Conference, 14–16 December 2010, Newport.

McAlpine, L. and G. Akerlind (2010). Rethinking Preparation for Academic Careers. In *Becoming an Academic: International Perspectives.* Eds. L. McAlpine and G. Akerlind. Basingstoke: Palgrave Macmillan, 155–170.

McAlpine, L., C. Amundsen and M. Jazvac-Martek (2010). Living and Imagining Academic Identities. In *Becoming an Academic: International Perspectives.* Eds. L. McAlpine and G. Akerlind. Basingstoke: Palgrave Macmillan, 125–154.

McInnis, C. (2010). Traditions of Academic Professionalism and Shifting Academic Identities. In *Academic and Professional Identities in Higher Education: The Challenges of a Diversifying Workforce.* Eds. G. Gordon and C. Whitchurch. New York: Routledge, 147–165.

Meek, V. L., L. Goedegebuure, R. Santiago, and T. Carvalho (Eds.) (2010). *The Changing Dynamics of Higher Education Middle Management.* Dordrecht: Springer.

Menger, P.-M. (2002). Portrait *de l'artiste en travailler. Metamorphoses du capitalisme.* Paris: Seuil.

Meyer, L. and I. M. Evans (2003). "Motivating the professoriate: Why sticks and carrots are only for donkeys." *Higher Education Management and Policy* 15(3): 151–167.

Middlehurst, R. (2010a). "Sustaining leadership in challenging times." *Higher Education Management and Policy* 22(3): 74–91.

Middlehurst, R. (2010b). Developing Higher Education Professionals. In *Academic and Professional Identities in Higher Education: The Challenges of a Diversifying Workforce.* Eds. G. Gordon and C. Whitchurch. New York: Routledge, 223–243.

Middlehurst, R. and J. Fielden (2011). *Private Providers in UK Higher Education: Some Policy Options*. Oxford, Higher Education Policy Institute (HEPI).

Miles, M. and M. Huberman (1994). *Qualitative Data Analysis*. London: Sage Publications.

Mills, D. (2010). Employment Patterns in and Beyond One's Discipline. In *Becoming an Academic*. Eds. L. McAlpine and G. Akerlind. Basingstoke: Palgrave Macmillan, 71–95.

Mitchell, W. J. T. (1995) 'Translator translated' (interview with cultural theorist Homi Bhabha), *Artforum*, 33(7): 80–84. http://prelectur.stanford.edu/lecturers/bhabha/interview.html (pp. 1–19).

Moron-Garcia, S. (2010). *Story to Set the Scene*. Conference on Academic Identities in the Twenty-First Century, University of Strathclyde, 16–18 June 2010.

Musselin, C. (2007). Transformation of Academic Work: Facts and Analysis. In *Key Challenges to the Academic Profession*. Eds. M. Kogan and U. Teichler. Kassel, Germany. UNESCO Forum on Higher Education and International Centre for Higher Education and Research, 175–190.

Musselin, C. (2010). The Impact of Changing Recruitment Practices on Academic Profiles. In *Academic and Professional Identities in Higher Education: The Challenges of a Diversifying Workforce*. Eds. G. Gordon and C. Whitchurch. New York: Routledge, 125–137.

Office for Public Management (OPM) (2010a). *New Models of Public Service Ownership. A Guide to Commissioning, Policy and Practice*. Public Interest Research Report. London: OPM.

Office for Public Management (OPM) (2010b). *Employee and User Ownership – Future Models for Public Service?* Public Service Briefing. London: OPM.

O'Meara, K. and R. E. Rice (2005). *Faculty Priorities Reconsidered: Rewarding Multiple Forms of Scholarship*. San Francisco: Jossey-Bass.

Paewai, S. R., L. H. Meyer and D. J. Houston (2007). "Problem solving academic workloads management: A university response." *Higher Education Quarterly* 61(3): 375–390.

Parker, J. (2008). "Comparing research and teaching in university promotion criteria" *Higher Education Quarterly* 62(3): 237–251.

Pepper, C. and W. Giles (2015). "Leading in middle management in higher education." *Management in Education* 29 (2): 46–52.

Pilkington, R. (2010). Reflecting on Complexity: Making the Journey into Staff and Educational Development – the Linguist's Tale. In *Creating a Profession: Building Careers in Educational Development*. Eds. S. Boon, B. Matthew and L. Sheward, SEDA Special Publication 27.

Pritchard, R. and J. Karlsen (Eds.) (2013). *The Resilient University*. Bern: Peter Lang.

Quick, K. and M. Feldman (2011). "Distinguishing participation and inclusion." *Journal of Planning Education and Research* 31(3): 272–290.

Rhoades, G. (2007) "Technology-enhanced courses and a mode III organization of instructional work." *Tertiary Education and Management* 13(1): 1–17.

Rothwell, A. and F. Rothwell (2014). Sustaining Academic Professional Careers. In *Academic Working Lives: Experience, Practice and Change*. Eds. L. Gornall, C. Cook, L. Daunton, J. Salisbury and B. Thomas. London: Bloomsbury, 129–137.

Sako, M. and Tierney, A. (2007). *The Future of HR: How Human Resource Outsourcing Is Transforming the HR Function.* Advanced Institute of Management Research: http://www.aimresearch.org.

Santiago, R. and T. Carvalho (2008). "Academics in a new work environment: The impact of new public management on work conditions." *Higher Education Quarterly* 62(3): 204–223.

Scottish Funding Council (York Consulting) (2007a). *Review of Shared Services and Collaborative Activities in Scotland's Colleges.* Edinburgh: Scottish Funding Council.

Scottish Funding Council (York Consulting) (2007b). *Review of Shared Services and Collaborative Activities in Scotland's Universities.* Edinburgh: Scottish Funding Council.

Sharafizad, F., Paull, M. and Omari, M. (2011). Flexible work arrangements: Accessibility in a university environment." *Australian Universities Review* 53(2): 43–58.

Shattock, M. (2009). *Entrepreneurialism in Universities and the Knowledge Economy: Diversification and Organizational Change in European Higher Education.* Maidenhead: Open University Press.

Shattock, M. (2014). University Governance in the UK: Bending the Traditional Model. In *International Trends in University Governance: Autonomy, Self-government and the Distribution of Authority.* Ed. M. Shattock. New York: Routledge, 127–144.

Sloan, K. (2011). *Managing Commercial Relationships and Skills Needed to Effectively Deal with the Business Sector.* Presentation to 9th HUMANE Winter School Alumni Network (WASN). 30 September 2011.

Smeenk, S., C. Teelken, R. Eisinga and H. Doorewaard (2008). "An international comparison of the effects of HRM practices and organisational commitment on the quality of job performances among European university employees." *Higher Education Policy* 21: 323–344.

Smith, C. and P. Boyd (2010). *Becoming an Academic: The Reconstruction of Identity by Recently Appointed Lecturers in Nursing, Midwifery and the Allied Health Professions.* Academic Identities in the Twenty First Century, University of Strathclyde, 16–18 June 2010.

Stensaker, B., J. Valimaa and C. Sarrico (Eds.) (2012). *Managing Reform in Universities: The Dynamics of Culture, Identity and Organisational Change.* Basingstoke: Palgrave Macmillan.

Stensaker, B. (2015). "Organisational identity as a concept for understanding university dynamics." *Higher Education* 69: 103–115.

Stevenson, H. and J. Mercer, (2011). *Challenging times: An analysis of current developments and future prospects for industrial relations in the UK higher education sector.* London: SRHE. https://www.srhe.ac.uk/downloads/StevensonMercerScoping Report.pdf.

Strike, A. (2010). Evolving English Academic Career Pathways. In *Academic and Professional Identities in Higher Education: The Challenges of a Diversifying Workforce.* Eds. G. Gordon and C. Whitchurch. New York: Routledge, 77–97.

Strike, A. and J. Taylor (2009). "The career perceptions of academic staff and human resource discourses in English higher education." *Higher Education Quarterly* 63(2): 177–195.

Stromquist, N., M. Gil-Anton, C. Colatrella, R. Obakeng Mabokela, A. Smolentseva, and E. Balbachevsky (2007). "The contemporary professoriate: Towards a diversified or segmented profession?" *Higher Education Quarterly* 61(2): 111–132.

Sun, P. and M. Anderson (2012). "Civic capacity: Building on transformational leadership to explain successful integrative public leadership." *The Leadership Quarterly* 23: 309–323.

Taylor, P. (2008) Being an Academic Today. In *Changing Identities and Voices in Higher Education*. Eds. R. Barnett and R. di Napoli. Abingdon: Routledge, 27–39.

Teichler, U., A. Arimoto and W. Cummings (2013). *The Changing Academic Profession: Major Findings of a Comparative Survey*. Dordrecht: Springer.

Teichler, U. and E. A. Hohle (Eds.) (2013). *The Work Situation of the Academic Profession in Europe: Findings of a Survey in Twelve Countries*. Dordrecht: Springer.

Tight, M. (2014) "Collegiality and managerialism: A false dichotomy? Evidence from the higher education literature." *Tertiary Education and Management* 20(4): 294–306.

Times Higher (2012). "Shared Services Centre is 'below standard' and new tasks won't help it improve, says STFC head." www.timeshighereducation.com/news/shared-services-centre-is-below-standard-and-new-tasks-wont-help-it-improve-says-stfc-head/420942.article.

Times Higher (2016). The University Workforce Survey: Results and Analysis. https://www.timeshighereducation.com/features/university-workplace-survey-2016-results-and-analysis.

Turnbull James, K. (2011). *Leadership in Context: Lessons from New Leadership Theory and Current Leadership Development Practice*. London: King's Fund. www.kingsfund.org.uk/leadershipcommission.

Universities and Colleges Employers Association (UCEA) (2008). *Where Are We Now? The Benefits of Working in HE*. London: UCEA.

Universities Scotland (2011). *Working Smarter. The Next Level of University Efficiencies*. Edinburgh: Universities Scotland.

UniversitiesUK (UUK) (2007). *Talent Wars*. Policy Briefing. London: UUK.

UniversitiesUK (UUK) (2011). *Efficiency and Effectiveness in Higher Education: A Report by the UniversitiesUK Efficiency and Modernisation Task Group*. London: UUK.

UniversitiesUK (UUK) (2015). *Efficiency, Effectiveness and Value for Money*. London: UUK.

University and Colleges Employers Association (UCEA) (2013). *Higher Education Workforce Survey*. London: UCEA. www.ucea.ac.uk/en/publications/index.cfm/hews13.

University and College Union (UCU) (2010). *Privatising Our Universities*. London: UCU.

University and College Union (UCU) (2013). *Making the Case against Outsourcing*. https://www.ucu.org.uk/media/5876/Fighting-privatisation-toolkit-Making-the-case-against-outsourcing/pdf/ucu_privtkit_makingthecase.pdf.

Watermeyer, R. (2015). "Lost in the 'third space': The impact of public engagement in higher education on academic identity, research practice and career progression." *Journal of Higher Education* 5(3): 331–347.

Watson, D. (2009). *The Question of Morale: Managing Happiness and Unhappiness in University Life*. Maidenhead: Open University Press.

Weerts, D. J., G. Freed and C. C. Morphew (2014). Organisational Identity in Higher Education: Conceptual and Empirical Perspectives. In *Higher Education: Handbook of Theory and Research*, 29. Ed. M. B. Paulsen. Dordrecht: Springer, 229–278.

Wenger, E. (1998). *Communities of Practice: Learning, Meaning, and Identity.* Cambridge: Cambridge University Press.

Whitchurch, C. (2013). *Reconstructing Identities in Higher Education: The Rise of Third Space Professionals.* New York: Routledge.

Whitchurch, C. and G. Gordon (2013). *Staffing Models and Institutional Flexibility.* London: Leadership Foundation for Higher Education.

Appendix
Details of the two studies

The Leadership Foundation study on Staffing Models and Institutional Flexibility

The study for the UK Leadership Foundation for Higher Education (Whitchurch and Gordon 2013) explored ways in which institutions are becoming more adaptive and flexible, and described opportunities and challenges associated with the adjustment of existing employment models and experimentation with new practices. It demonstrated how local managers such as heads of department have a critical role to play in implementing policy at local level, and suggested how they might be supported in this. It also showed how institutions work with different staffing models for different activities and functions, and cope with tensions that may arise. Although the study was focused on the UK, international commentators were consulted where it was known that new approaches to staffing models were being considered and/or implemented.

Seven case institutions were selected after discussions with the Leadership Foundation and senior commentators in the higher education system about institutions where there was evidence of innovative practice. For this reason the seven institutions were not intended to be representative of the system as a whole, although an even balance was sought between pre- and post-1992 institutions, and in relation to geographical spread, to reflect the impact of history and locale. The institutions included:

- Three pre-1992 institutions, two of which were members of the Russell Group
- Three post-2004 institutions, two of which were involved in partnerships, and the third a specialist institution
- One private institution

Two of the institutions were in Scotland, three in the south of England and two in the midlands.

The study drew on two sets of qualitative interviews:

A. With sixteen 'expert witnesses' in higher education and other sectors in the UK (10), Hong Kong (4), Ireland (1) and the US (1), who acted as system commentators. These included vice-chancellors, pro-vice-chancellors with a people management remit, heads of administration, directors of human resources, and representatives of unions, the UK-based UniversitiesHR (the national association of directors of human resources) and the Committee of University Chairs. The witnesses were selected initially from discussions with the Leadership Foundation and with professional bodies, and also via early interviews with the witnesses themselves. Each one brought expertise and experience in specific areas of interest, often from more than one institution, and were able to provide a system-wide view. The interviews in Hong Kong were specifically targeted at the use of different staffing models in relation to non-Hong Kong University Grants Committee-funded academic activities, an area which the government is encouraging to serve a growing student demand. A further interview was carried out in Ireland because the government there had made significant proposals with respect to changes that would affect staffing models and practices (Department of Education and Skills 2011); and one with a US commentator who had a national level perspective on changing staffing patterns and conditions of work. They were asked:

   • What do you see as the main issues/priority areas in relation to the roles and careers of academic faculty and those involved in learning support activity?
   • Are you aware of thinking about more flexible employment models (of whatever scale)?
   • What sort of initiatives are you aware of? Which of these are in use and what progress has been made with them?
   • What are the perceived benefits and what are the challenges created by such models?
   • What has triggered changes in practice (e.g. changed market positioning; mergers; funding cuts)?
   • What principles might underpin thinking about more flexible models e.g. equity?
   • What do you think are significant trends for the future?
   • Do you think that faculty expectations have been affected by recent changes? If so, in what ways?
   • Should and do line managers have a degree of discretion, for example on workload allocation, or when hours are worked?
   • How do you think sensitivities around these issues with members of academic faculty and unions can be ameliorated?
   • Can you point us to specific institutions where interesting practices are occurring?
   • Are there other general points that you think could be usefully raised in our study?

B. With thirty-seven senior and middle managers in seven institutions in the
    UK, including vice-chancellors; pro-vice-chancellors; heads of administra-
    tion; heads of other functions such as human resources, academic services
    and estates; deans and heads of school; academic managers; members of
    governing bodies and representatives of partner institutions. They were
    asked:
    • What are the main issues in relation to academic faculty and those
       responsible for academic support activity in your institution?
    • What are your key priority areas?
    • Are you/your institution thinking about more flexible employment
       models in relation to academic faculty and those involved in academic
       support activity (of whatever scale)?
    • What sort of initiatives are you aware of? Which of these are you/your
       institution using and what progress have you made with them?
    • What are the perceived benefits and what are the challenges you face?
    • What principles underpin your thinking about more flexible models e.g.
       equity?
    • What has triggered changes in practice (e.g. changed market positioning;
       merger; funding cuts)?
    • What developments in other higher education institutions/other sectors
       are most influencing you?
    • What do you think are significant trends for the future?
    • Do local managers have a degree of discretion, for example on workload
       allocation, or when hours are worked?
    • Do you think that individual expectations of the institution, particularly
       those of academic faculty, have been affected by recent changes? If so,
       in what ways?
    • How have you ameliorated potential sensitivities with academic faculty
       and unions about changes in practice?
    • Are there other general points that you think could be usefully raised in
       our study?

The Higher Education Academy Project on Shifting Landscapes: Meeting the Staff Development Needs of the Changing Academic Workforce

The Higher Education Academy (HEA) project (Locke, Whitchurch et al
2016) aimed to develop a broader understanding of teaching, research and
learning support roles and careers, associated development needs in relation to
promotion and transition across and between them, and the variables affecting
these such as institutional contexts and career routes. It constructed evidence
of the 'lived experience' of faculty and learning support staff, shifts in their
careers and work, and ways in which they and their institutions might address
these opportunities, for instance via reward and recognition mechanisms. It
explored the needs and aspirations of those with 'teaching-only' contracts,

provided evidence of the type of support offered to those new to higher education, and considered the extent to which this contributed to morale and motivation and career development.

University College London Institute of Education was commissioned by the UK Higher Education Academy to explore the following research questions:

- What do UK Higher Education Statistics Agency (HESA) and other data tell us about the changing academic career paths and staff transitions with respect to differing institutional contexts, discipline influences and career routes for teaching-only, research and learning support pathways?
- What opportunities exist for reward and recognition among those contracted only to teach in different types of institution?
- What kind of support is offered to those new to higher education in research, teaching and teaching-related roles, and to what extent does this contribute to morale and motivation and support career development and alignment to the UK Professional Standards Framework (UKPSF)?

The main source of quantitative data for the project was the HESA staff data (HESA 2015). These were analysed to identify trends in the higher education sector and the institution-specific backdrop to the case studies. This analysis was complemented by longitudinal analysis of comparable data from earlier years and survey results from other sources such as the Higher Education Funding Council for England (HEFCE), the Universities and Colleges Employers Association (UCEA) and the University and College Union (UCU).

Eight case study institutions were selected in consultation with the Higher Education Academy on the basis of national location (five English and one each from Scotland, Wales and Northern Ireland), institutional type (e.g. Russell Group, post-1992 university) and proportion of those who, according to the HESA data, had teaching-only contracts.

The study also drew on two sets of qualitative interviews:

A. With 6–7 academic or learning enhancement staff. These included one early career academic member of staff, one mid-career academic member of staff, an individual with a teaching-only contract, an individual with a research-only contract, an individual with a traditional teaching and research remit and an individual with a learning support remit. They were asked:

Past
1.1 Could you talk me through how you came to be in your current role?
- What was the subject of your first degree? Postgraduate study?
- Previous posts?
- Have you worked outside the HE sector?

1.2 Were there significant turning points in your career and what were these?

1.3 Were there any factors that have helped or hindered you in developing your career?

Present

2.1 Could you describe your work in your current role (e.g. teaching and research, teaching-only, research-only, learning support)? If the latter, can you be more specific?
- How many years have you been in your current role?
- Who is your current line manager (e.g. Head of Department)?
- Could you estimate what proportion of your time you spend on teaching and research, and any other key areas of activity you have mentioned?

2.2 What reward and incentive mechanisms are available to staff in your institution (e.g. access to discretionary increments, promotion, career development)?

2.3 What formal or informal professional development opportunities are available to you, within or external to your institution?
- Are there any institutional career pathways within your institution?
- Are there any key relationships inside or outside your institution that are important for your professional development?

2.4 Are you aware of the UK Professional Standards Framework? If so, do you feel that it is relevant to the type of work you do?

Future

3.1 What are your career aspirations for the future?

3.2 In what ways does your institution support the aspirations of academic staff generally, and more specifically the aspirations of teaching-only, research-only and learning support staff? What else might the institution do to support such staff?

3.3 Is there anything else you would like to say that might be relevant to our study?

B. With 1–2 members of the senior management team. These included one director of human resources or pro-vice-chancellor to provide an overview of the institution and its strategies in relation to the professional development of faculty. They were asked:

1 Can you describe your current role at the university in relation to staff management and development?

2 Could you describe in broad terms the University's approach to staffing?
- How does this relate to the University's overall strategy and mission?
- Would it be possible for you to provide copies of any relevant policies and strategies?

3 Can you give an overview of trends in staff patterns at the University, such as the balance of teaching and research staff and teaching-only staff?

4 What formal or informal professional development opportunities are available to academic staff generally, and more specifically to teaching-only, research-only and learning support staff, within or external to your institution?
- For example, study leading to qualification/award?
- Study or training not leading to a qualification? Being mentored?
- Presenting at seminars/conferences?
- Authoring of published papers/monographs?

5 What reward and incentive mechanisms are available to academic staff generally, and more specifically to teaching-only, research-only and learning support staff in your institution?
- Access to discretionary increments?
- Promotion? Would it be possible for you to provide a copy of your policy or criteria around promotion? Can people be promoted for teaching or other work such as knowledge exchange?
- Career development?
- Institutional teaching awards? Application for National Teaching Fellowships?

6 In what ways does your institution support the career aspirations of academic staff generally, and more specifically of teaching-only, research-only and learning support staff? What else might the institution do to support such staff?
- For example, are there any specific career development initiatives (e.g. knowledge exchange or community engagement pathways)?

7 Could you tell me about any factors you see as helping or hindering teaching-only, research-only and learning support staff in developing their careers?
- At your institution or in the higher education sector more broadly?
- Is it possible to move from a teaching-only post to a teaching and research post? How often does that happen?

8 Are you aware of the UK Professional Standards Framework? If so do you feel that it is relevant to the work of academic staff at your University?

9 Is there anything else you would like to say that might be relevant to our study?

Note in relation to the selection of institutions in both studies: in the UK, the Further and Higher Education Act 1992 removed the binary line between the universities and former polytechnics, so that convention now distinguishes between those which existed prior to the Act and those created at any point afterwards. After 1992, in the enlarged university sector, institutional groupings emerged based on similarities of profile and ethos. The first of these was the Russell Group of leading research-intensive universities.

Index

community networks 23
competition between universities 6
Connectors 71
consortia 6, 13, 55, 56, 127 *see also*
  collaboration; partnerships
constructive alignment 105
consultancy work 115–17
contracts: adaptive approaches 18;
  creating discursive space 155–6;
  expectations outside term time 133;
  construction of facilitative relationships
  136; flexibility versus insecurity
  122; formal xiii, 7, 9, 18, 135, 140,
  144, 161; informal xiii; interface
  of structures and relationships 53;
  middle managers and renewal of 86–7;
  negotiating framework 7; *private sector*
  approach 57; 'relational' 38, 46–7;
  stretching of time and space 150–4;
  structural challenges to relationships
  132–3; transactional and relational
  46–7; typology of relationships 140;
  UK higher education workforce 10–11;
  see also annualised contracts; open-
  ended contracts; part-time work or
  contracts; psychological contract; short-
  term contracts; teaching and research
  contracts; teaching-only appointments
  or contracts; zero hours contracts
cost of living adjustments 57
cost-benefit analysis 40, 60, 65,
  142, 158
costs 7, 55–6
creativity and innovation 53
Crosby, B. C. 53
Csikszentmihalyi, M. 48
culture change 41, 138
culture of feedback 91
Cummings, W. 26–7

deans 7, 20, 46, 177
Delanty, G. 4
department(s) xiv, 3, 4, 16, 20–1, 25,
  34–7, 39, 47, 49–50, 52, 68, 75–6,
  80–85, 87–8, 91–93, 95, 100, 106,
  108, 110, 113–114, 119, 123–5,
  132–3, 135–7, 140–2, 144, 148, 150,
  155–6, 158, 161–2

development and training *see*
  professional development
directors of human resources 15, 49, 73,
  129, 149, 155, 161, 176
disciplinary base changes 8, 62
disciplinary networks 131–2
discretionary awards 64, 88, 137
discretionary relationships 140–3
discretionary time and space 38, 136
discursive approach 124, 159
discursive space 154–7
diversification of roles and relationships 8
doctorate 26, 30, 74, 106
Duberley, J. 28

emergent practices, bottom up 105;
  interacting activity systems 118–20;
  mentors 107–8; networks 108–15;
  external networks 110; networking
  and social capital 113; portfolio working 115–17; teams 105–7; *see also*
  relationships, reconstructing; *specific*
  practices
emergent practices, top down 18, 122;
  consortia and partnerships 126–8;
  employment package 122–5;
  intentions and practice 147–50;
  outsourcing 125–6, 128–30; private
  providers 131–2; shared services
  125–8; structural challenges
  to relationships 132–3; *see also*
  relationships, reconstructing; *specific*
  practices
empirical studies 14–15 *see also* case
  studies
employability xiv, 6, 7, 9, 10, 12, 24,
  26, 30–1, 46, 55, 61, 63, 74, 76,
  94, 106, 108, 149–50, 161; *see also*
  careers
employee partnership model 55–6 *see*
  also partnerships
employment contracts *see* contracts;
  specific types
employment 'flexicurity' policies 10
employment model interpretation 84,
  157–8 *see also* workload models
employment package as a whole 122–5
Engeström, Y. 118, 129, 160

relational contracts 46–7; unions and 125
'public engagement' 26, 63, 76
pure research (Mode 1) 7

Rast, D. 52
reactive approach 63–65, 69–71
reconstructing relationships *see* relationships, reconstructing
re-employment models 55
regenerative approaches 9
regulatory obligations 35
'relational' contracts 38, 46–7
relationships 3, 47–53; actor-network theory 4–5; vis-a-vis agendas 160–1; changing interface with structures 53–4; constructive alignment 105; creating discursive space 154–7; culture change and 41; day-to-day xiv, 3, 5, 9, 17, 23, 46, 91, 92, 108, 142, 144, 157, 161; disproportionate effects of 3, 88, 89, 99, 153, 160, 162; facilitative 95, 135–138; formal 4, 17, 51, 92–3, 105, 117, 142, 147; informal 4, 17, 105–6, 132, 138, 142, 147, 156; institution-individual interface 13–14; *instrumental* and *investing* 143–4; 'mature relationships' 160; mutual respect in 133; new relationships in changing contexts 22; *obligatory, discretionary* and *voluntary* typology 140–3; organisational 3, 5, 50; outsourcing, impact of 129; overlapping networks 3; with peers 68; potential for positive change 160–1; potential institutional synergies 22–3; 'social partnership approach' 48; spatial 4; with states or governments 3–4; integration of strategy and practice 51; stretching of time and space 153; structural challenges 132–3; between structures and relationships 20–3, 37–40; working relationships xiii, 10, 15, 45–61, 131, 141, 158 *see also* institutional structures and relationships; networks; teams

relationships, actor-network theory *see* actor-network theory
relationships, implications of workload models 32–3 *see also* workload models
relationships, reconstructing 135; construction of facilitative relationships 135–8; iterative process 135, 138; case example of listening institution 138–40; typology of relationships 140–4
relationships, and social capital *see* social capital
relationships and people management *see* human resource management; people management
research: creating discursive space 155–6; fluid definitions 152; future considerations 7, 157; influence on academic roles 6; *integrated* approach 54; teaching activities in 'own time' 142; pedagogic 11, 54, 83, 123; portfolio work 115–17; *private sector* approach 57; pure and applied (Mode 1 and Mode 2) 7; scholarship and 11, 54, 83, 123; tensions with teaching activity 147; value accorded to teaching versus 78–80; *see also* knowledge transfer; teaching and research contracts
Research Evaluation Framework (REF) 65, 74, 93, 136
research funding 6, 7
research-only contracts 11
rewards and incentives 33–4; discretionary payments 64, 88; equity issues 124; construction of facilitative relationships 137; 'favour' and 'gift' economies 142–3; *integrated* approach 54; middle manager influence 87, 88; *partnership* approach 55; *private sector* approach 57; 'soft' mechanisms 123–4; staff involvement in policy development 148; teams 138; top down initiatives 123–4; *see also* promotion and progression; motivation
risk 53, 161
roles, academic *see* academic roles